THE CLAIM

Dwight K. Nelson

THE CLAIM

Nine radical

claims of Jesus

that can revolutionize

your life

Dwight K. Nelson

Pacific Press Publishing Association
Boise, Idaho
Oshawa, Ontario, Canada

Edited by Marvin Moore
Designed by Dennis Ferree
Cover photo by © Sinclair Studios
Typeset in 10/11 Caslon

The author assumes full responsibility for the accuracy of all facts and quotations cited in this book. Unless otherwise noted, all Scripture quotations are from the New Revised Standard Version of the Bible.

Library of Congress Cataloging-in-Publication Data

Nelson, Dwight K., 1952-
    The claim : nine radical claims of Jesus that can revolutionize your life / Dwight K. Nelson.
        p.   cm.
    Includes bibliographical references.
    ISBN 0-8163-1236-2
    1. Bible. N.T. John—Devotional literature. 2. Jesus Christ—Words—Meditations. 3. Christian life. I. Title.
BS2615.4.N45   1994
226.5'06—dc20   94-26480
                                                        CIP

94 95 96 97 98 • 5 4 3 2 1

Contents

For Karen
"You whom my soul loves"
Canticles 1:6

Preface

They've been around in America now for almost four decades; and thanks to our exploding export business in entertainment, nearly every inhabitant on earth (well, almost) has had the chance to decide whether to love them or not. Since I don't know your private convictions on the matter, allow me to risk sharing mine with you. Not wishing to blatantly announce that I can't stand them, perhaps it would be more accurate—and charitable—for me to declare that I can't *under*stand them.

I'm referring to the popular television daytime soap operas, those melodramatic and never-ending serial programs that play across the afternoon channels of American television (and now around the globe "As the World Turns," so to speak) day after day after day.

You've seen them, haven't you? The brightly lighted, gaudily decorated drama sets across which will traipse the heavily made-up "soap" stars whose teary love stories and quick-healing tribulations have become the mesmerizing fare of millions of viewers every weekday afternoon. America's great soap operas.

But the greatest riddle of all is, Why call them "soaps"? Be honest, now: Can you name a single person who ever watched one of them and got clean in the process? Soap is for cleansing. But not so the "soaps"!

THE CLAIM

So why call them soap operas at all?

I asked that question once out loud and was duly informed about a "trivial pursuit" bit of entertainment history I apparently hadn't mastered while growing up. The original daytime soap operas were sponsored by American soap manufacturers. As a result, the TV programs earned the nickname "soap operas," a two-bit epithet that has stuck through the decades of their popular reign. (Though I have yet to find anyone who's gotten clean watching them!)

Fortunately for me, though, you don't have to watch them to know what's been happening on them! The local newspaper where I live here in southwestern Michigan carries a Saturday-morning week-in-review for the ten most popular daytime soaps. And in a few choppy sentences, you can get more than an adequate feel for the upended world the soaps represent.

Take, for example, this review of a single week on the well-known and widely watched soap "All My Children":

> Julia apologized for coming on too strong with Charlie, who was surprised to learn that Maria is her sister. Julia complained to Charlie that Maria interferes in her life. Dimitri warned Kendall that Erica wouldn't be happy if she learns the girl is looking for Richard. [Whew! How's a soul supposed to keep track of *all* these children?] Charlie refused when Dimitri wanted to hire him to find Richard, but Hayley agreed to take the case. Erica was furious when she returned home and found the memorabilia that Kendall had collected on her father, Richard Fields. Hayley lied to Erica that she isn't helping Kendall look for Richard. Dixie and Tad

jumped into bed together after admitting they're still in love. [Did you know that 94 percent of the sexual relationships on these soaps take place outside of marriage?] Dixie said she doesn't expect Tad to leave Brooke and Jamie to be with her (*South Bend Tribune*, 25 September 1993).

It appears that whoever the "my" is in "All My Children" has just been bequeathed more than a heart-full of headaches from all these love-crossed children, and all this in only a single week of programming! Clearly, it's going to take more than soap to wash them clean.

But then, soap can't wash them clean, can it? For in a moment of self-disclosing candor, don't we all have to admit that the titillating excesses of America's daytime soap operas are, in fact, the sordid enlargements of our own national and personal portraits? The fact is that when you tune in on weekdays between noon and 3:00 p.m., you can vicariously experience all our societal excesses and extremes as well as relive all our own private dysfunctions and decay.

For behind the pasty makeup and crocodile tears of "The Bold and the Beautiful" is a shared chapter or two in the life story of each of us. And while the world may think we're having the "Days of Our Lives," we still can't mute the persistent whispers of a gnawing conscience, can we? For it's not only "The Young and the Restless" who are restlessly and oftentimes hopelessly caught in the moral webs of their own spinning.

But forget about the soaps! Faced with the quiet desperation of our own real-life dramas, how shall we answer the groping question that haunts us in the twilight shadows of the twentieth century: How can we ever be set free—how will we ever be washed clean?

THE CLAIM

What follows in this short volume is the answer that lies embedded in the heart of a revolution whose time has come for America. And for you and for me. The Jesus Revolution. Because the last hope left for the America of these soaps is the Jesus of this revolution. The revolutionary Jesus of Nazareth, whose two-thousand-year-old teachings are the only hope left for our dizzying life in the fast track of the nineties. And why not Jesus? We've tried everything else. Just look at the soaps! And nothing's worked till now. So why not the Jesus Revolution?

But this little book isn't a collection of all His teachings. Instead, it's a concise, contemporary examination of nine of the most radical claims He ever made. For within these nine radical claims is found the very secret to the moral freedom and inner cleansing we've secretly been searching for all along. All nine radical claims are found in the short and colorful Gospel of John—a story so compellingly simple that a child can understand it, yet so deeply profound that philosophers and sages have yet to fully comprehend it.

And so to the Jesus of John we must turn. For therein lies what humankind ultimately seeks—a forever kind of freedom with a deep and lasting cleansing. Freedom for our shackled lives, cleansing for our sullied hearts.

And accomplishing that, you must admit, would be nothing short of a revolution! But then, that's Jesus for you. The one revolution in life that's really *for* you.

Dwight K. Nelson
Berrien Springs, Michigan
Easter, 1994

CHAPTER
1

"The Young and the Restless"

I AM the water of life

Her life was a soap opera, and she moved with the young and the restless. For she was both. You know the type—the fidgety, pretty-faced woman who can't bite her shiny manicured nails, so she taps her well-heeled toe restlessly beside the cosmetic counter. Not that she really needs any more of that pricey makeup magic. But there are always those driven souls who keep trying to make a good thing better. Until they finally make it worse.

But as you stare into those haunted dark eyes, you could swear you've seen her face before, that pale and picture-perfect oval, exquisitely manicured but heavily mascaraed. It is the very same mask that waltzes across the production set of "The Young and the Restless."

Only this woman can't make believe that her life is make-believe any longer. Oh, sure, she's got a cover-girl face. But she hides a covered-up life too. And all the neon eyeliner and crimson blush and purple-painted lips in the world could never hide the truth.

The truth about the woman with a pretty face and a fast life and a barren heart. Burned out to a smoldering heap. So that all she has left are ashes from a sooty string of failed romances. And it doesn't take a psychologist to figure out that the woman has crashed and burned in the familiar flight pattern of the young-and-restless life cycle: first, you're used up—and then you're tossed out; turned on—and then burned out. Hollowed out until there's nothing left inside but a smoldering ash heap.

She is a cover-girl face with a covered-up life. Young. And restless. And hopeless. But a life that is about to be uncovered forever and ever. Amen.

Not that she's praying at this moment, mind you. After all, when you live with the bad news she's been making, what's there to pray about anymore? Although if she prays at all, she surely prays for a friend. Because pretty faces don't usually make many friends. And you know it's *really* bad when the only friend you have is a man who's not your own.

Why do you think she's coming here at noon? Simple. Because there will be nobody here to ignore her, nobody here to shame her, nobody here at all. She may be the envy of every woman and the desire of every man in town, but she's also the butt of every gossip as well. So you can be certain there is a method to her young-and-restless madness in coming to the village well in the heat of the day. She risks meeting nobody at noon. The biddies come in the morning or evening, and the men don't come at all.

So she catches her breath when she sees a stranger seated upon the mossy lip of that ancient well. And a man—a Jewish man, at that! Which is double trouble for a Samaritan woman.

But Jesus never says a word. His eyes may be smiling, but His lips are silent. He just watches, as the now-nervous covergirl, whose eyes refuse to meet His, quietly lowers her empty water jar on the end of a goat's hair rope down a hundred feet to the cool waters of Jacob's well.

"The Young and the Restless"

The jar splashes into the depths below, gurgling its echoes up to the mouth of the well. And when it feels taut and full, the woman slowly hoists it back up, hand over hand, until its brimming rim glistens in the noon-day sun.

She's about to leave as quietly as she arrived, when a voice stops her. "Could I have a drink of water, please?" And in that quiet favor is the birthing of a brand-new story for the young and the restless. A beginning that may be just as new for you too.

Read John's quick-sketch record of that moment. "A Samaritan woman came to draw water, and Jesus said to her, 'Give me a drink.' (His disciples had gone to the city to buy food.) The Samaritan woman said to him, 'How is it that you, a Jew, ask a drink of me, a woman of Samaria?' (Jews do not share things in common with Samaritans.)" (John 4:7-9).

"*You* are asking a drink from *me*?"

The woman knows that for a Jewish male, she has two strikes against her—three, if the stranger only knew! Strike one, she is woman. Had not the rabbis written: "One should not talk with a woman on the street, not even with his own wife, and certainly not with someone else's wife, because of the gossip of men." And, "It is forbidden to give a woman any greeting."

Strike two, she is Samaritan. The animosity between Jews and Samaritans was notoriously deep-rooted, festering back to the origins of the Samaritans as a mixed race of half-breeds during the long-ago days of the Assyrian Empire. The Jews had a proverb, "The only good Samaritan is a dead one."

And strike three? Well, fortunately, the stranger doesn't know that she's lived a soap-opera life as a woman of ill repute. After all, she assures herself, he *never* would have broached this conversation had he

THE CLAIM

known her stained and sullied strikeout secret.

But still the cover-girl face is astonished that this very evidently Jewish male is asking to actually touch her cup of water and drink its contents. "I can't believe you're even asking me!" she exclaims.

To which Jesus quietly replies, " 'If you knew the gift of God, and who it is that is saying to you, "Give me a drink," you would have asked him, and he would have given you living water' " (verse 10).

Gazing into those dark and haunted eyes, there is no question what Jesus is telling her: "You may be thinking about My parched and thirsty lips—but I am talking about your parched and thirsty life." He offers her "living" water; she thinks He means "flowing" water!

Quick is her retort: "Hey, now, wait a minute, Mister. It's impossible for you to give me flowing water when you're sitting right here on the edge of our village well. Why, you can't even get into the well! So where's this 'flowing' water you speak of? Who do you think you are, anyway? You think you're greater than our ancestor Jacob, who dug this well, do you? Or do you know about some secret spring we haven't heard of?"

The Stranger waits through her interrogation. And then pointing down the well shaft, Jesus answers, " 'Everyone who drinks of this water will be thirsty again, but those who drink of the water that I will give them will never [literally, "no, not forever"] be thirsty. The water that I will give will become in them a spring of water gushing up to eternal life' " (verses 13, 14).

There's no mistaking Him now! It may have sounded like He was speaking of "flowing" water the first time she heard Him, but this time, in rapid-fire sequence, Jesus' pointed spiritual symbols come pounding unmistakably on the door of the young and the restless heart! It is crystal clear that He speaks now of gushing water that lasts forever and ever. Amen.

But she isn't ready for the "Amen" quite yet. Because right now, she has the sexual and social and spiritual dimensions of her life all mixed up. And all she can think about is, *It sure would be great not to have to come here in the heat of the day to keep on avoiding the women and men of this town* (that's her social side). *And what's more—if I had this magic water, I could stay at home with my man* (her sexual side) *and never come back to this horrible place again! God, I want that water* (her spiritual side)!

And so the cover-girl face exclaims to Jesus, " 'Sir, give me this water, so that I may never be thirsty or have to keep coming here to draw water' " (verse 15).

Jesus stares into the pretty face and knows that behind that masked pain there is a woman who will never understand the metaphor of eternal life until she admits her desperate spiritual need. And so He speaks into her eyes now, "I want to give you that water. In fact, I want to give it to you and your husband, so go home and get him. And then I'll give this water to you both."

For one split second, she holds His gaze, and then instinctively she lets her eyes fall, as they have a thousand times before. Her blush is perfectly concealed by her quick-thinking quip: Oh, you won't have to wait at all, because I don't have a husband at all.

She looks back up—her plastic smile is tight but true. And her eyes snap back: So quit asking questions and gimme the water.

Jesus never misses a beat either. Holding her gaze, He raises His voice slowly but forcefully like a prophet: "You're right, Madam. You don't have a husband. You've had five husbands, and the man you're sleeping with now doesn't even belong to you!"

15

THE CLAIM

An ashen face is followed by a scarlet blush. "Oh, wow, you're a prophet!" Gulp. "Say, I've always wanted to meet a man of the cloth." And with that, her words turn tail and ditch straight into a dry theological debate.

And the gentle Stranger who has targeted her life for eternity quietly chases after her heart. And in a masterful stroke of divine persistence, Jesus pursues her full circle until she comes face to face with the Messiah! Because Jew and Samaritan alike both passionately prayed for the promised Deliverer.

"The woman said to him, 'I know that Messiah is coming' (who is called Christ). 'When he comes, he will proclaim all things to us.' Jesus said to her, 'I AM he [literally, I AM], the one who is speaking to you'" (verses 25, 26).

You want the Messiah? Well, I AM He. You want everlasting water? Well, here I AM. In the original language of the Gospel of John, Jesus' answer is two words long: I AM.

I AM He. There it is—the first of nine radical I AM claims in John. Looking into that intense cover-girl face, Jesus replies: "Look, Lady—I AM what you've been looking for; and I AM who you've been longing for. I AM the water of life, so come to Me and drink."

If only the young and the restless of today knew the healing truth of that quiet offer. "I AM the water of life, so come to Me and drink."

But I'm afraid we are all like the Samaritan woman. Drinking and drinking and drinking—but never slaking our thirst.

Could it be that the words of the ancient prophet were destined to include us all? God speaks: "My people . . . have forsaken me, the fountain of living water, and dug out cisterns for themselves, cracked cisterns

"The Young and the Restless"

that can hold no water" (Jeremiah 2:13).

Living as you and I do in a world of parched and painful dreams and brittle and broken lives, wouldn't it be the height of insanity for us to cling to our cracked cisterns and broken water jars while Jesus stands before us, beckoning us to a gushing spring of living water? His offer isn't only for her! " 'Let anyone who is thirsty come to me, and let the one who believes in me drink. As the scripture has said, "Out of the believer's heart shall flow rivers of living water" ' " (John 7:37, 38). Come and drink, come and drink!

But where do we turn to slake our thirst, we who are the inheritors of the young-and-restless Samaritan woman? Could it be that, like her, we drink from the broken cistern of sexual abandon? I received an anonymous letter, written to me by a student in the university where I pastor. May I share a line or two of this anonymous pain with you?

Dear Pastor,

I wish I could shout it out to so many of the fellow students on campus. Please, stay away from sex until you are within the protective, loving boundaries of marriage. It hurts so much to realize that everything you could experience with your wife [or husband], in every God-inspired, imaginable way, you have already done with someone else, or a variety of people for that matter. . . .

The T.V., for example, teaches us that sex is fun, and promiscuity is acceptable, and can be a happy occasion. WRONG. I found, and firmly believe, that God implanted a law in every human heart, that we violate every time we enter

17

through the gates of life prematurely. I have yet
to meet the person who can tell me that having
had sex with a person he or she is not wedded
to was an enriching experience.

And were this anonymous letter from a broken cistern to end there, it would remain a bleak commentary
on the reality of life on this planet. Who is a stranger to
such shorn hopes and broken dreams? But the unknown
student ends his letter with a blush of new hope:

> God forgives, and I can now forgive myself. How-
> ever, the scars are still there, and it will take
> time to heal. The scars stay and the barren,
> empty well of God-given sensuality takes time
> to fill up. I would urge all . . . to think and go for
> the unparalleled, long-term reward that's await-
> ing them.

Did you catch that language? "The empty well of
God-given sensuality takes time to fill up." But He can
fill you up again. The One who filled up that woman
long ago still promises, Come and drink of My water,
and you shall never ("no, not forever") be thirsty again!

And so for every burned-up and tossed-out heart today, there is good news: The same Jesus—who gave
the cover-girl face at the well a new beginning—stands
ready to accept you too! Never mind your covered-up
life. He has water that can cleanse those covered-up
stains, sexual or otherwise, and make you clean again.
His Book is full of promise:

> If we confess our sins, he who is faithful and
> just will forgive us our sins and cleanse us from
> all unrighteousness (1 John 1:9).

"The Young and the Restless"

> Come now . . . says the Lord: though your sins
> are like scarlet, they shall be like snow; though
> they are red like crimson, they shall become
> like wool (Isaiah 1:18).

> Who is a God like you, pardoning iniquity and
> passing over the transgression? . . . You will cast
> all our sins into the depths of the sea (Micah
> 7:18, 19).

The only condition? Like the woman at the well, you must come to Him and drink.

But then, of course, sexual abandon isn't the only broken cistern we carry with us down the dry and dusty thoroughfares of life. How about the cracked water jar of intellectual pride or the broken cistern of ego-driven self-dependence that thrives in a society like ours?

The truth is that we all face the temptation of becoming too big for our own britches or dresses. And none of us is exempt from overblown egos. "I did it my way" isn't an exclusive temptation in Frank Sinatra's private domain!

But it is also a fact that intellectual pride and ego-driven self-dependence are a cracked pot. And they're a broken jar with a masterful disguise. Because, of course, like the U.S. Army commercial intones, you must "be all that you can be." Nobody can gainsay our God-given right (and responsibility) to develop ourselves to the best of our abilities. But leaning very hard on the laurels of our own accomplishments is like sucking on a straw in a brackish stagnant pool: you never get enough, and it always makes you sick.

" 'Everyone who drinks of this water will be thirsty again, but those who drink of the water that I will give them will never be thirsty. The water that I will give will become in them a spring of water gushing up to eternal life' " (verses 13, 14). I AM the water of life, so come to Me and drink.

Which is good advice, by the way, for those of us tempted to drink at the broken cistern of financial thirst. Because the thirst for wealth can never be slaked.

Last fall I read a short book, *The Plague of the Black Debt*, written by two Oxford graduates and economists who have charted the sixty-year cyclical history of financial depressions. They are predicting a massive economic collapse before the end of the 1990s, possibly even by 1995 or 1996. According to their economic prognostications, accompanying this financial collapse will be a rise in urban violence and a disintegration of social structures, both nationally and globally.

Now, I am not an economist, and I cannot judge the veracity of their predictions, though I must admit to being duly impressed with the track record of their financial predications over the last decade or so. But you don't have to be a financial wizard to realize how utterly tentative our economy remains. One false move in the financial world, and this house of cards can come toppling down, and all we'll be left with will be the broken cisterns and cracked jars of our empty financial holdings!

The same Jesus at the well would later in His life predict a global economic collapse just before His return to this planet (see Luke 21:25-27). So no wonder He appeals for us to store up our treasures in heaven and invest ourselves in the kingdom of God (see Matthew 6:19-21, 33).

The thirst for financial security will never be slaked. For cruel is the nature of wealth's incessant pursuit: While you are driven to invest more and more in yourself, you are left feeling less and less secure about yourself and your future. Such is the fickle end to the relentless pursuit of mammon!

Of course, a man ought to provide for his family, and a woman ought to prepare for her future. But when halfway around the world twenty thousand lives can be extinguished in the grip of an overnight killer quake and the rest of India's nine hundred million survive on the edge of extinction, maybe we ought to rethink our definitions of financial security and personal comfort.

Has money become a broken cistern for us?

" 'Everyone who drinks of this water will be thirsty again, but those who drink of the water that I will give them will never be thirsty. The water that I will give will become in them a spring of water gushing up to eternal life' " (John 4:13, 14).

You see, what Jesus said to the woman at the well, He says to all the young and not-so-young and restless of heart. I AM the Water of Life, so come to Me and drink.

By the way, that woman and her entire neighborhood took Jesus up on His invitation and came to Him to drink. Their response is a final clue as to what it means for us to come and drink too: "Many Samaritans from that city believed in him because of the woman's testimony, 'He told me everything I have ever done.' . . . They said to the woman, 'It is no longer because of what you said that we believe, for we have heard for ourselves, and we know that this is truly the Savior of the world' " (verses 39, 42).

And that's what it means to come and drink. It simply and quietly means to believe that Jesus is your Saviour too. God knows we have tried everything else. So why not turn to this Stranger at the well, this I AM Messiah who makes the greatest thirst-quenching offer in the world? You'll never be thirsty again, is His unmistakable, unsurpassable promise.

How can He make such a radical offer?

Months later, when this same Jesus hung pinned and crushed beneath three Roman nails on a cross atop a hill called Golgotha, a legionnaire of the emperor lifted his lance and plunged it into His lifeless chest. And when the soldier withdrew his spear from Jesus' side, "at once blood and water came out" (John 19:34). The symbolism is too vivid to be missed. The water that flowed on Calvary spilled from the side of the One who said, I AM the Water of Life—so come to Me and drink.

Someone died for you and me long ago so that in that fountain of flowing love atop Calvary we might gaze upon the only One who today can still cleanse our souls and quench our thirsts.

The question begs, then, to be asked: What do *you* think about this same Jesus? Never mind, for now, the woman with the cover-girl face and her neighbors, who all concluded that He "is truly the Savior of the world" (John 4:42). Who is Jesus to you?

The great German theologian of this century, Karl Barth, once declared that what a man or a woman thinks about Christ will ultimately determine what he or she thinks about everything else.

He's absolutely right.

So what do *you* think about Jesus?

It happened in Kent, Washington. James Wilson decided he wanted a well to augment the water supply on his five-acre tract of land. So he hired J. C. Maxwell, a professional well digger, to drill a hole deep into the earth behind the Wilson home and hopefully find water.

It was a Tuesday when the well digger arrived and began to sink his steel shaft into Mother Earth. Ten feet down, no water. Twenty feet down, no water. Fifty feet and still no water.

"Shall I dig on, Mr. Wilson?"

"Of course! We must have water."

Seventy-five feet down, no water. One hundred feet, no water. Deeper and deeper the metal bit chewed its way to the heart. One hundred twenty-five feet, one hundred fifty feet, one hundred ninety feet. Finally, the drill crunched its way to two hundred feet below the surface. Still, no water.

"Farther, Mr. Wilson?"

"Yes!"

And at two hundred ten feet down, there arose from the bosom of the earth a faint and distant sound to the two men high above. It was a deep, throaty gurgling sound of roaring, rushing water! Wilson and Maxwell instinctively stepped back from the hole—just in time to witness an explosion of water that shot out of the ground like Old Faithful herself! It was a geyser into the sky, and nobody could stop it!

Neighbors with shovels were summoned. Drainage ditches were dug. A mechanical digger was placed in operation. And still the water exploded into the heavens from beneath the earth!

They had struck an artesian well. And that was on Tuesday.

By Wednesday evening there was such a flood of water that Mr. Wilson called the sheriff for more help. County road equipment was brought in. Irrigation ditches were dug to serve the entire valley.

Geologists brought onto the scene estimated that water was pouring out of that well at the rate of 1,600 gallons per minute! It was an outpouring of water that they estimated would adequately serve forty-six thousand persons a day! They had struck an artesian well that would never run dry.

THE CLAIM

" 'Everyone who drinks of this water will be thirsty again, but those who drink of the water that I will give them will never be thirsty. The water that I will give will become in them a spring of water gushing up to eternal life' " (verses 13, 14).

Isn't it time that you strike that well too? Never thirsty again—what a way to begin a revolution!

CHAPTER
2

"As the World Turns"

I AM the bread of life

Pause for a moment and listen to three voices—a conservative American Jew, a Polish Roman pope, and a popular evangelical psychologist. Listen carefully, for you may agree with them in the end that "as the world turns" today there is a moral famine that is sweeping our globe, and human civilization is rapidly starving to death.

First, consider this biting commentary that appears in a new book, *A Jewish Conservative Looks at Pagan America*, written by Don Feder:

> When a rap song that calls for the murder of cops climbs to the top of the charts; when taxpayers are told that their objections to subsidizing a photograph of one man urinating into the mouth of another constitute censorship (when critics consecrate the same as the highest expression of the aesthetic); when a state's voters come within a hair's breadth of legalizing medical murder in the name of relieving suffering; when a presidential candidate informs voters that whether or not he violated his marriage vows is none of their business, *we may as well declare intellectual bankruptcy and have*

THE CLAIM

the nation placed in moral receivership (*Discipleship* 77 [1993], 16, emphasis supplied).

I don't know if Pope John Paul II would put it quite that way, but there is no question that he, too, believes there is a moral famine raging across the face and soul of a starving civilization. And he made the news all over our nation (and probably the Western world) when he released his tenth and newest papal encyclical, *Veritatis Splendor* ("the splendor of truth"). In this 183-page document, the pope writes of a "genuine crisis" in church and society, "an overall and systematic calling into question of traditional moral doctrine" (*Veritatis Splendor*).

The pope strongly asserts the church's ability to identify and teach basic morality and to require Catholic theologians to agree to these judgments. So strongly does the pontiff feel that, according to the Associated Press, he came within a hair's breadth of "invoking the language of papal infallibility." (In fact, in a draft of this encyclical—six years in the making—that circulated this past summer, the language of infallibility was apparent but was removed before the release.) The pope himself emphasizes "that this is the first time such an authoritative and extensive outline of fundamental moral principles has ever come from the papacy."

What does it mean? Simply that there is a growing consensus in religious circles that we are faced today with a monumental moral famine that is ravaging the land.

Consider, now, the voice of a conservative Protestant evangelical psychologist named James Dobson, president of Focus on the Family. In a recent newsletter, Dr. Dobson and coauthor Gary Bauer described the moral famine this way:

Traditional teachings of the church are contra-
dicted daily in the classroom [of public schools].
Parents have lost the right even to know when
their daughters have aborted a baby. Condoms
are distributed willy-nilly by school officials.
Venereal disease is rampant. Language is so foul
it is even decried by the secular press. Ultimately, the faith for which parents would give
their lives is undermined and weakened among
the young. It's all here! Again I say, this is the
theater of war that will establish the course of
Western civilization for centuries to come. And
we are losing it! (*Focus on the Family Newsletter*, October 1993).

Whether we agree or disagree with the theological
and political agendas of these three authorities, most
of us would concur that all three voices are indeed right
in their pointed assessments of a moral famine in our
starving world. "As the world turns," human civilization is in deep trouble. One hardly needs to be religious at all to concur!

So in a world that morally has turned inside out,
where shall we turn? Hasn't the time come to turn to
Jesus' second radical claim in the Gospel of John? After all, without its revolutionary promise, there can be
no healing for our desperate moral famine!

There He sits, cross-legged on the sprawling grassy
hilltop. The afternoon sun is warm, and gentle winds
ascend from the shimmering waters below. It would be
a most pastoral scene, this picture of the handful of
them seated there on the soft green carpet, were it not
so smelly! Because the sea breezes off the distant Lake
Tiberius blow the pungent aroma of dead and drying
fish.

THE CLAIM

You can smell them from up here, those scaly and spiny creatures spread out near the beached and water-logged fishing skiffs that caught them, spread out beneath the blazing afternoon sun that dries them.

But it isn't the fishy sea breeze that has Jesus' attention right now. Instead, He stares into the hazy distance and sees them coming—a crowd one biblical estimate places at five thousand. But since that estimate includes only the men, the crowd actually may have exceeded ten thousand people!

"When he looked up and saw a large crowd coming toward him, Jesus said to Philip, 'Where are we to buy bread for these people to eat?' He said this to test him, for he himself knew what he was going to do" (John 6:5, 6).

The hilltop where Jesus and His twelve disciples are resting is within walking distance of a lakeside village called Bethsaida, and Philip happens to hail from that sleepy town. So when Jesus turns to him, it's as if He is saying, "Look, Phil, you live around these parts. What do you think? Is there anywhere nearby where we can do some grocery shopping for this multitude headed toward us?"

Poor Philip is overwhelmed by the very thought of that shopping list! And when he answers Jesus, he exclaims that the immediate problem isn't finding a grocery store, but rather, "We simply don't have the money for so mammoth a supper!"

But in this familiar story from the life of Christ, it's the disciple Andrew who overhears the exchange between Jesus and Philip and offers a temporary stop-gap solution. " 'There is a boy here who has five barley loaves and two fish. But what are they among so many people?' " (verse 9)

It is then that the unforgettable drama unfolds. For

Jesus quickly stands and gazes out over the growing sea of people who now cover the grassy hillside above Galilee. And picking up the box lunch of an anonymous lad, Jesus lifts it to the God of heaven in thanksgiving and then proceeds to hand out a fish-and-bread supper to every hungry stomach on that slope that late afternoon!

And the Gospel reads that they all received "as much as they wanted" (verse 11). But then, that was Jesus. And that *is* Jesus—still the only One who can stand up in the midst of our gnawing hungers and feed us to our deepest satisfaction.

Which was why some quick-witted political scientist in the crowd that evening came up with the bright-eyed idea, This man needs to run for president! Like wildfire, the proposal caught on, and en masse the crowd rushed the hilltop.

"When Jesus realized that they were about to come and take him by force to make him king, he withdrew again to the mountain by himself" (verse 15).

Which still remains a very good idea, by the way. For when the world wants to make you a star, a hero or a heroine, it's time to get away and be alone with God again. Because if you fall victim to their hypnotic chant, it'll kill you morally and spiritually. And besides, the kind of heroes the world wants isn't the kind a starving civilization really needs! So quit wasting your time trying to make it big in a world that'll make you small. The moral giants of history have always been the women and men who rejected the clamor of fame and chose a life of faithfulness instead. Jesus did that evening.

But the punch line of the story really comes the next day, when the crowd tracks Him down and finds Him out. This time, they're more than a little ticked! After being rebuffed so forcefully the evening before, they're not sure they want to believe in this "maybe Messiah."

"So they said to him, 'What sign are you going to give us then, so that we may see it and believe you? . . . Our ancestors ate the manna in the wilderness' " (verses 30, 31). There isn't an unsubtle bone in their bodies! The crowd heatedly challenges this Miracle Worker. "All right, so you gave us bread for supper. What we want to know is, Can you do better than barley? How about some real live manna!"

You see, among the Jews of Christ's day, it was believed that when the true Messiah appeared, he would repeat the miracle of Moses in the wilderness and cause manna to come down from heaven. Angel food cake for everybody, so to speak!

Jesus looks into their confused and disturbed faces and cries out, "You have it all wrong." The coming of the Messiah isn't about angel food manna. It's about life-giving Bread!

" 'For the bread of God is that which comes down from heaven and gives life to the world.' They said to him, 'Sir, give us this bread always.' Jesus said to them, 'I AM the bread of life. Whoever comes to me will never be hungry, and whoever believes in me will never be thirsty' " (verses 33-35).

There it is again: I AM—the explosive couplet that Jesus reserved for His most radical claims. And what is His claim this time? Remember last time, how Jesus used a double negative with the woman at the well—"You will *no not* ever be thirsty again"? Well, today with the crowd, He offers a triple negative—"You will *no not never* be thirsty or hungry again!" You get the impression, don't you, that this Bread of Life really truly satisfies? You will *never, never, never* be hungry again!

Period!

However, Jesus isn't quite ready for the *period* yet,

because He is saving His punch line to the end! And you must read it.

But be warned! What you're about to read will seem repulsive to your very Western and proper sensibilities. But if we hastily dismiss these following words, we, too, will die in the moral famine that is already destroying our starving world. So consider carefully Jesus' punch line:

> "I AM the living bread that came down from heaven. Whoever eats of this bread will live forever; and the bread that I will give for the life of the world is my flesh."
>
> The Jews then disputed among themselves, saying, "How can this man give us his flesh to eat?"
>
> So Jesus said to them, "Very truly, I tell you, unless you eat the flesh of the Son of Man and drink his blood, you have no life in you. Those who eat my flesh and drink my blood have eternal life, and I will raise them up on the last day; for my flesh is true food and my blood is true drink. Those who eat my flesh and drink my blood abide in me, and I in them" (verses 51-56).

That is as graphically repulsive as you can get! Unless, of course, you've read Piers Paul Read's bestseller, *Alive: The Story of the Andes Survivors*, billed as "the greatest modern epic of catastrophe and human endurance." It is the riveting account of an Uruguayan rugby team that on October 12, 1972, boarded an old Fairchild F-227 chartered plane and took off for a much anticipated football match across the Andes mountains in neighboring Chile. Tragically, the planeload of forty-five passengers never arrived in Santiago. Flight No. 571 went down in the killing snows of one of the world's highest mountains.

Their only shelter was the plane's shattered fuselage, their only supplies were a little wine and some bits of candy, and for the world that gave up after eight days of frantic searching, they were gone. Missing. Dead atop the Andes, was the final news bulletin.

But there were actually thirty-two survivors. And the harrowing account of how that diminishing number of athletes ended up surviving at all is what turned the world's heart and stomach ten weeks later when, in the end, sixteen stragglers descended from the summit of death.

> Finally, Canessa [one of the kickers] brought it out into the open. He argued forcefully that they were not going to be rescued; that they would have to escape themselves, but that nothing could be done without food; and that the only food was human flesh. . . . Canessa did not argue just from expediency. He insisted that they had a moral duty to stay alive by any means at their disposal. . . . "It is meat," he said. "That's all it is. . . . All that is left here are the carcasses, which are no more human beings than the dead flesh of the cattle we eat at home" (Piers Paul Read, *Alive: The Story of the Andes Survivors*, 76).

In the end, Canessa's logic carried the day and saved the lives of sixteen rugby players. They crawled off the mountain alive because they had subsisted on the flesh of their fallen comrades.

Cannibalism in any form is repulsive to human thought. Yet Jesus speaks in such unmistakable language: " 'Very truly, I tell you, unless you eat the flesh of the Son of Man and drink his blood, you have no life in you' " (verse 53).

What in the world is Jesus calling for?

It's hardly surprising that the Jews reacted the way they did! According to their liturgical and ceremonial laws, to drink blood from any creature was anathema. Although, if they had stopped to think for a moment and had recalled the reason they had been commanded by God not to drink that blood, they would have had the one clue that unlocks Jesus' radical and cryptic claim!

You see, the law of Moses was clear: "You shall not eat the blood of any creature, for the life of every creature is its blood" (Leviticus 17:14). Blood is a symbol of life. Which means that if they hadn't been so hasty to interpret Jesus' radical claim literally, they would easily have understood what Jesus was saying—that to drink His blood and to eat His flesh meant to absorb His life. It was all a graphic metaphor!

You and I use that same metaphor all the time. We "devour" books, we "drink in" a lecture or a scene. We "swallow" a story and sometimes even "swallow" an insult. We "ruminate" (chew the cud) on an idea or a poem, or we "chew on it" for a while. We talk about "stomaching" something that was said or find ourselves unable to do so. And sometimes we even have to eat our own words! As George Beasley-Murray concludes, "I have heard fond grandmothers declare they could 'eat up' their grandchildren (i.e., love them to death!), whereas to bite someone's head off conveys a very different notion" (*John* in Word Biblical Commentary, 99).

Jesus is no different when He binds up His second

radical claim with the metaphor of eating and drinking.

What is He really talking about? " 'I AM the living bread that came down from heaven. Whoever eats of this bread will live forever; and the bread that I will give for the life of the world is my flesh' " (verse 51). There is no question what Jesus' radical words are really claiming. When He speaks of giving His flesh on behalf of others, He is sharing with us a graphic and unforgettable depiction of how His life will, in fact, end.

It is more than coincidental that the opening words of this lengthy chapter in John remind us that when Jesus made this radical claim, it was the Passover season. For it would be but one Passover later that He would be pinned between heaven and earth, His flesh nailed up, His blood spilled and dripping on a lone cross outside the gates of Jerusalem. There is no question that He who is the Bread of Life is at the same time declaring Himself to be the Lamb of God. The Passover Lamb, who became the broken Bread.

Thus it is that Jesus cries out to anyone who will listen: When you see My flesh broken and My blood spilled out, as you will atop Calvary, then you will know that the Bread of Life has been broken for the world. Bread broken for you. Take that Bread and eat of it, and you will never, never, never be hungry again.

As a nation, we, with our young President Clinton, have wrestled over our moral obligation of whether to keep U.S. military forces in that faraway, famined land of Somalia. For who can forget the bloodshot and haunted eyes of the Somalian children that stared back at us from the glossy pages of our weekly news journals? Those bone-protruding specters of grotesquely stretched skin over their forlorn little skeletons, what shall we do for them, we who must stare into the bony, hollow faces of death by starvation?

But as tragic as those bloated bellies and protruding ribs are, we can no longer afford to ignore an even more devastating famine in the land.

An old sycamore farmer turned prophet named Amos described our age to a T—"The time is surely coming, says the Lord God, when I will send a famine on the land; not a famine of bread, or a thirst for water, but of hearing the words of the Lord. They shall wander from sea to sea, and from north to east; they shall run to and fro, seeking the word of the Lord, but they shall not find it" (Amos 8:11, 12).

The famine has already struck, and our society is starving to death! How else can we describe the inane and insulting humor we feed upon via the crude antics of two animated characters the world knows as Beavis and Butthead? That a nation of such affluence and promise can find solace in such mindless fare is proof enough that a moral famine rages across the land.

No longer content with our quest for reality, we have now plunged into the Orwellian horrors of "virtual reality." Unplugging our minds from facing up to our mounting intellectual and moral bankruptcy, we now have invented the ultimate technology: A computerized mind control that can lead the unsuspecting human psyche into the shadow lands of unbridled fantasy. Or, as *Time* magazine put it, "With virtual sex, smart drugs and synthetic rock 'n' roll, a new counterculture is surfing the dark edges of the computer age" (8 February 1993, 58).

We are starving to death. Can anybody help us?

Yes, cries the revolutionary Jesus of the Gospels. I can help you, for I AM the Bread of Life. And what you hunger for most of all is what I can offer you best of all. Come to Me and eat and drink of Me.

THE CLAIM

But what do You mean, Jesus? we wonder aloud.

Consider the words of German commentator A. Schlatter:

"What we have to do with his flesh and blood is not chew and swallow, but that we recognize in his crucified body and poured out blood the ground of our life, that we hang our faith and hope on that body and blood and draw from there our thinking and our willing" (quoted in George Beaseley-Murray, 95).

Did you catch that? "That we hang our faith and hope on that body and blood and draw from there our thinking and our willing." Simply put, in order for the Bread to be eaten, we must go to where the Bread was broken. Which means that the only reality left for our starving hearts and our empty lives is the ultimate reality of Calvary's center cross.

No virtual reality there. Rather, at the cross you and I are confronted with the shining truth about the God who loved us more than He loved Himself. " 'For God so loved the world that he gave his only Son, so that everyone who believes in him may not perish but may have eternal life' " (John 3:16). Were the truth of that ultimate reality to sink into our minds and penetrate our little worlds, there would never be a moral famine again!

For how did the John of the Gospel put it near the end of his life? "Perfect love casts out fear" (1 John 4:18). And is it not our fear of boredom, our fear of having to face the more than virtual reality of our guilt-ridden lives, our fear of meaninglessness and worthlessness—is it not our pantheon of fears that drives us to pursue such bankrupt and barren caches of morally moldy bread? The "perfect love" that shines from the cross is the very Bread of Life that alone can stave our hunger and satisfy our souls.

This is the stuff of a revolution! For why would we want to chase any longer after the paltry crumbs and dried crusts of this world's virtual best if we could feast on the Bread of Life with His full-filling love that restores a deep sense of worth and meaning to our lives once more? Knowing that we are loved to the depths of Calvary's kind of love, there would be no reason to go chasing any longer after the moldy slices of society's almost virtual but never quite real fare!

But the value of bread is not in its shelf life. Bread is best when it's consumed. And that is Jesus' offer: " 'I AM the living bread that came down from heaven. Whoever eats of this bread will live forever' " (John 6:51).

So why not find a quiet corner tomorrow morning where you can be alone with the Bread? Remember, in order for the Bread to be eaten, you must go to where the Bread was broken. Pull out that dusty Bible again, and find the story of the cross in one of the four Gospels (Matthew 26, Mark 15, Luke 23, and John 19). Quietly read and relive that crimson moment when the Bread of Life became broken for you and me. And hold the picture of that relentless love in your heart's eye. Whisper to your heart, He did it all for me, because He loves me. And after a few contemplative moments, get up and go out and face the world that waits for you. You will discover that having eaten of the Bread of Life, your old collection of gnawing hungers (what never could—and never will—fill you anyway) will be gone.

For "as the world turns," the revolutionary truth remains: "I AM the Bread of Life." Very good news for a starving world. For at the cross of Jesus there is no famine.

CHAPTER
3

"One Life to Live"
I AM God

Here's a trick question for you: Have you ever been an alcoholic? The reason that's a trick question is because it is impossible to answer that question with a Yes! No human being can say, Yes, I once *was* an alcoholic. For it is now an uncontested truth that once you become an alcoholic, you will remain an alcoholic for the rest of your life. Yes, of course, a *reformed* or *recovering* alcoholic, to be sure. But nevertheless, an alcoholic.

I have a little black book in my library entitled *Twenty-Four Hours a Day*. It's a year's worth of daily readings, written especially for recovering alcoholics. It's part of the Alcoholics Anonymous strategy of keeping reformed alcoholics faithful to the life of sobriety that they've chosen to seek. And so whether you're an alcoholic or not, here's what you would read on the morning of June 1:

Some things I do not miss since becoming dry: that over-all awful feeling physically, including the shakes, a spliting [sic] headache, pains in my arms and legs, bleary eyes, fluttering stomach, droopy shoulders, weak knees, a three-day beard, and a flushed complexion.

38

Also, facing my wife or my husband at break-fast. Also, composing the alibi and sticking to it. Also, trying to shave or put on make-up with a shaky hand. Also, opening up my wallet to find it empty. *I don't miss these things, do I?*

And, of course, the answer to the rhetorical question is certainly intended to be No! For who would miss a life of such despair? But this small volume isn't only about a despair that is past. It also describes a joy that is present. And on June 4 you would read the following words:

> Some things I like since becoming dry: feel-ing good in the morning; full use of my intelli-gence; joy in my work; the love and trust of my children; lack of remorse; the confidence of my friends; the prospect of a happy future; the ap-preciation of the beauties of nature; knowing what it is all about. *I'm sure that I like these things, am I not?*

And of course, what recovering alcoholic wouldn't exclaim Yes! Why, just this last week I was chatting on the sidewalk with one of my parishioners. And when the conversation had ended and we were heading to-ward our cars, he turned around and called to me, "And by the way, Pastor, it's been almost two years. And I haven't had a single drop!" The grin on his face was confirmation enough—"I'm sure that I like these things, am I not?"

But forget about alcoholics for a moment. Here's a second question for you: Have you ever been a sinner? Just like the first question above, this one is just as tricky. Because if your answer is Yes, then it means you still are. For the truth about life on this planet is that once a sinner, always a sinner. (Oh yes, like the alcoholic, it is possible to be a recovering and reformed sinner, but a sinner nonetheless.)

Which makes us sinners and alcoholics very much alike, does it not? Because there's no difference between us. No difference in the degree of our struggles. No difference in the scars from our battles for freedom. No difference at all.

I don't know your personal story. But after twenty years of pastoring, I know our shared journey. And I know that there is a whole planetful of us with battered-down and bloodied-up lives. You'd never guess it, looking into our well-manicured faces. With our smiling masks that keep parroting the reply, "Fine, thank you, and you?" in answer to "How're you doing?" nobody could possibly guess that our marriage is in shambles or our kids are in counseling or our careers are in receivership! After all, if there's anything our society has taught us, it is to always look like a blossoming success! (Though more often than not we feel like "blooming idiots," trying so hard to look like what we're not!) But we go on trying, miserably trying, don't we? Defeated, discouraged, depressed, and downright despondent—with only "one life to live," who hasn't thought about giving it all up?

Which is why some of us as alcoholics or as sinners do—give up, that is. Longing for spiritual freedom, we languish in moral failure.

So the question begs to be asked by alcoholics and sinners anonymous and alike: Is there any hope, any secret that can turn a *conquered* alcoholic into a *conquering* one . . . any hope, any secret that can turn a *vanquished* sinner into a *victorious* one?

For every "one life to live," the good news is that

there is hope! Hope wrapped up in a secret only two words long—two words in English, two words in the Hebrew, two words in the Greek—the two most liberating words ever spoken! And for all of us with only "one life to live," these may become the two most important words we shall ever discover!

"Jesus said to them, 'Very truly, I tell you, before Abraham was, I AM' " (John 8:58). I AM. There they are again—only this time they stand all alone.

And what do they mean, those two little words? There was absolutely no question in the listeners' minds! Look how they reacted! "They picked up stones to throw at him, but Jesus hid himself and went out of the temple" (verse 59).

And John, the writer of this Gospel, leaves no mystery as to why they attempted to stone Jesus. His unmistakable clue is planted later in the narrative of another crisis moment: "The Jews took up stones again to stone him. Jesus replied, 'I have shown you many good works from the Father. For which of these are you going to stone me?' The Jews answered, 'It is not for a good work that we are going to stone you, *but for blasphemy, because you, though only a human being, are making yourself God*' " (John 10:31-33, emphasis supplied). No question the Jews understood the meaning of Jesus' two words, I AM!

Because they all knew the story!

Ever watch a pile of dry autumn leaves burn? The word isn't *burn*, is it? It's more like *erupt* or *explode!* Especially if you've got a stiff October wind blowing.

My mother always worried about my becoming a pyromaniac, because I was utterly fascinated with fire as a boy. And I still am, I must confess! For who doesn't enjoy the thrill of watching that enormous pile of dry, brittle fallen leaves explode into a roaring orange ball of flame! You almost hate to see the pile incinerated so quickly.

But then, that's what is supposed to happen when you burn up leaves—they become consumed and turn to ashes. Which is why Moses can't believe his eyes. Because the leaves *aren't* burning up! Only they're not in a raked pile; they're growing on a bush. A bush that simply refuses to burn up in that roaring orange conflagration. Wide-eyed, with gaping mouth, the wilderness shepherd draws closer to this amazing spectacle!

Read it for yourself, this story the Jews—who almost stoned Jesus—knew so well:

> [Moses] looked, and the bush was blazing, yet it was not consumed. Then Moses said, "I must turn aside and look at this great sight, and see why the bush is not burned up." When the Lord saw that he had turned aside to see, God called to him out of the bush, "Moses, Moses!" And he said, "Here I am." Then [God] said, "Come no closer! Remove the sandals from your feet, for the place on which you are standing is holy ground." . . . And Moses hid his face, for he was afraid to look at God (Exodus 3:2-6).

But once Moses got a handle on his quaking heart, he was able to calm his voice long enough to ask the name of this Voice that called to him from the burning bush. And "God said to Moses, 'I AM who I AM' " (verse 14).

The Jews all knew the story of Exodus 3. And when Jesus stood before them and dramatically declared, " 'Before Abraham was, I AM!' " they knew exactly what He was claiming to be—the great I AM God of the Old Testament, the Self-existent and Eternal One, the great

Creator God of the universe, the God of the burning bush!

And so they took up stones to kill Him!

And what shall *we* do with Jesus' incontrovertible claim to divinity, we who live two millenniums later? For it is very evident; we can't miss it—He is claiming to be God! So shall we stone Him too?

Oh no, not us. And, besides, that would be too violent, too bloody, and too messy. And so the rocks we hurl are of a much more sophisticated nature. We stone Him with our silence, our stony, stony silence. After all, trying to survive as we are in the fast track of the nineties, who has time anymore for this same Jesus?

No, we wouldn't stone Him. Dismiss Him, maybe. Ignore Him, belittle Him, forget Him, reject Him, maybe. But not stone Him.

But why? Could it be we still don't know who He really is? How shall we answer the old King James query: "What think ye of Christ?" (Matthew 22:42)?

There is no point in trying to prove the divinity of Jesus Christ right here. Fact of the matter is, there's no need to. For we have just read His own claim to divinity, a claim that He exercises in the opening story of John's same chapter—the tale of the woman caught in adultery. Ever read it?

The early-morning sun is streaking its golden rays through the dusty air of the temple portico, air glistening with the dust of a thousand sandals that have choked their way into the sunbathed courtyard of Jerusalem's temple. They've come early, the masses of the Holy City, because they want to see Jesus.

He doesn't disappoint them as He climbs a few marbled steps higher so the crowd can hear Him. There, beneath the early-morning sky, Jesus does what He always did whenever He had a crowd. He tells them

stories about their Father in heaven, stories of a relent-
lessly loving Father whose outstretched arms will always welcome home every runaway boy and girl (see
Luke 15:11-32).

Breathlessly, the multitude listens to this warm reci-
tation of divine love, when suddenly, with an angry explosion, the morning tranquility is broken by the sounds
of loud, raucous voices. The crowd instinctively parts
in respectful deference to the voices of the temple
leaders, the religious hierarchy of Jerusalem.

But the ecclesiastics don't come alone. They half push
and half drag a young woman. Shoving her before Jesus,
their haughty sneers announce, " 'Teacher, this woman
was caught in the very act of committing adultery.' "
The crowd gasps; the woman sobs. " 'Now in the law
Moses commanded us to stone such women. Now what
do you say?' " (John 8:4, 5). It is a masterfully sprung
trap.

And Jesus knows it. Because if He decides that the
woman should not be stoned, the prelates will turn to
the crowd and crow, "Ah-hah, we told you the young
preacher has no respect for the law! Abandon him, one
and all!" But if Jesus decides that she should be stoned,
off to Pilate, the Roman governor, the clergy would race,
decrying this young rebel teacher who seeks to take
the law into his own hands. A clever trap, really. Because Jesus is damned if He says Yes and destroyed if
He says No.

So He says nothing. "Jesus bent down and wrote with
his finger on the ground" (verse 6). And when His
secret inscriptions in the dust of the temple floor are
finished, Jesus stands and faces His accusers. " 'Let anyone among you who is without sin be the first to throw
a stone at her' " (verse 7).

You see, an ancient tradition has it that what Jesus

was inscribing on the dusty marble were the secret sins of each of the church elders. Which, in the end, only proves the truth Jesus modeled about His Father. For God is in the business of shaming and embarrassing no one! With His finger, He writes the Ten Commandments on stone that can never be effaced or erased (see Exodus 31:18). And no wonder, for the law of God is really a portrait, a transcript of His eternal character of love. And so the Decalogue He carves with His finger upon the stone. So that we will never forget it or Him.

But our sins, yours and mine and the church elders' that sunlighted morning, where does He record the stained and sullied secrets of our lives? On a trampled floor, written in dust, so that with the first whiff of a morning breeze our secrets are blown quietly away. We have His promise: "I, I AM he who blots out your transgressions for my own sake, and I will not remember your sins" (Isaiah 43:25).

Impatient with Jesus' apparent doodling on the floor, the clerics step up and peer over the Master's shoulders. Ashen faced, they read their own private exposés, and without a word, "they went away, one by one, beginning with the elders; and Jesus was left alone with the woman" (verse 9).

The crowd is breathless. What will the Teacher say to the adulteress? "Jesus straightened up and said to her, 'Woman, where are they? Has no one condemned you?' She said, 'No one, sir.' And Jesus said, '*Neither do I condemn you.* Go your way, and from now on do not sin again' " (verses 10, 11, emphasis supplied).

Did you catch that? The only One who was without sin and who could have thrown a stone at her, didn't. He forgave her, instead.

And " 'who can forgive sins but God alone?' " (Mark 2:7).

45

THE CLAIM

C. S. Lewis, in his classic apology of the Christian faith, *Mere Christianity*, masterfully "proves" the divinity of Jesus by focusing on His "claim to forgive sins—any sins":

> Now unless the speaker [offering forgiveness] is God, this is really so preposterous as to be comic. We can all understand how a man forgives offenses against himself. You tread on my toe and I forgive you, you steal my money and I forgive you. But what should we make of a man, himself unrobbed and untrodden on, who announced that he forgave you for treading on other men's toes and stealing other men's money? Asinine fatuity [stupidity] is the kindest description we should give of his conduct. Yet this is what Jesus did. He told people their sins were forgiven, and never waited to consult all the other people whom their sins had undoubtedly injured. He unhesitatingly behaved as if He was the party chiefly concerned, the person chiefly offended in all offenses. This makes sense only if He really was the God whose laws are broken and whose love is wounded in every sin (55).

" 'Neither do I condemn you. Go your way, and from now on do not sin again.' " " 'Very truly, I tell you, before Abraham was, I AM.' So they picked up stones to throw at him" (John 8:11, 58, 59).

Lewis concludes:

> A man who was merely a man and said the sort of things Jesus said would not be a great moral teacher. He would either be a lunatic—

on the level with the man who says he is a poached egg—or else he would be the Devil of Hell. You must make your choice. Either this man was, and is, the Son of God: or else a madman or something worse. You can shut Him up for a fool, you can spit at Him and kill Him as a demon; or you can fall at His feet and call Him Lord and God. But let us not come with any patronizing nonsense about His being a great human teacher. He has not left that open to us. He did not intend to (ibid., 56).

"Before Abraham was, I AM."

So the question repeats itself, What difference does Jesus' claim to divinity, to be the Eternal God, the great I AM—what difference does that claim make in your life?

A few months ago, one of my parishioners slipped by the mailbox in front of our home and dropped this letter off without a stamp:

Dear Pastor,

I have just returned from a Twelve Step meeting. It has been a year since I attended. I have been attending church most of my life. I'm sad to say that today I felt like I was where I belonged—the other hurting people with their experiences of healing with the help of God did me more good than the past year in church. . . . I wish this was not true. Through the divorce I only felt further wounded. . . . I have not found [in the church] the support, help, love and caring through the hellish pain I have been through and continue to experience

as a human being. . . . I know that God loves
me and will be with me always.

Sincerely,

And with that, she signed her name and ended her
letter. A letter about pain in the wider community but
healing in a small Twelve Step group.

You're acquainted with the Twelve Step recovery
movement that has swept our nation, aren't you? In
practically every burg and village, there now meets one
of these small therapy groups, each a small part of a
burgeoning international movement.

It all began back in the 1930s with Bill Wilson and
Dr. Bob Smith—two men who were on the brink of
self-destruction. But, as they would later describe it,
both their lives were miraculously and dramatically
transformed. And out of their joyful recovery was born
the vision to reach out to fellow sufferers by forming
themselves into therapy groups for mutual healing and
help.

The successful birth of Alcoholics Anonymous six
decades ago has been reproduced in the conception
and delivery of numerous other Twelve Step siblings.
Groups such as Narcotics Anonymous, Gamblers
Anonymous, Sex and Love Addicts Anonymous,
Overeaters Anonymous, Abusers Anonymous,
Workaholics Anonymous. Maybe one of these days
someone will start a Sinners Anonymous, and then we
all can join!

Who are these twelve-steppers? They are the anonymous group faces of our own pain and hurt and dysfunction and failure and sickness and despair. And most
of the groups are built upon the familiar Twelve Steps
of Alcoholics Anonymous:

"One Life to Live"

1. We admitted we were powerless over alcohol—that our lives had become unmanageable.

2. Came to believe that a Power greater than ourselves could restore us to sanity.

3. Made a decision to turn our will and our lives over to the care of God as we understood Him.

4. Made a searching and fearless moral inventory of ourselves.

5. Admitted to God, to ourselves, and to another human being, the exact nature of our wrongs.

6. Were entirely ready to have God remove all these defects of character.

7. Humbly asked Him to remove our shortcomings.

8. Made a list of all persons we had harmed, and became willing to make amends to them all.

9. Made direct amends to such people wherever possible, except when to do so would injure them or others.

10. Continued to take personal inventory and when we were wrong promptly admitted it.

11. Sought through prayer and meditation to improve our conscious contact with God as we understood Him, praying only for knowledge of His will for us and the power to carry that out.

THE CLAIM

12. Having had a spiritual awakening as the result of these steps, we tried to carry this message to alcoholics, and to practice these principles in all our affairs.[1]

I am grateful for the healing these Twelve Steps—in their myriad forms—have brought to men and women, young and aged. As a pastor I have witnessed the reality of those recoveries, for I have known individuals who have indeed found new freedom and life through these movements. I believe God uses this recovery method.

But it is imperative that all twelve-steppers (and you may be one of them) and all sinners anonymous (and you and I are certainly among them—so much for our anonymity!)—it is imperative that you and I and all of us recognize that *there is only one Higher Power that can liberate our lives!*

Step 3 calls Him the "God as we understand Him." But John 8 calls Him Jesus Christ, the great I AM! It may take twelve steps to recover the body and mind. *But it takes a final step to redeem the heart and soul.* For the goal of the human quest is not just recovery; it must also be redemption! And only one Person can redeem us!

So here is the final step: "Jesus said to the Jews who had believed in him, . . . *'You will know the truth, and the truth will make you free.'* . . . *'So if the Son makes you free, you will be free indeed'* " (John 8:31, 32, 36, emphasis supplied).

Which makes this final step the best news of all! For if your life is being held in bondage today by some addiction or dysfunction, by some guilt or fear, by some failure or hopelessness that has overpowered you, you

---

[1]Reprinted with permission of Alcoholics Anonymous World Services, Inc.

can experience lasting freedom and lifelong healing from the One who still declares, "I AM!"

"I AM your forgiveness"—that's what Jesus told the woman at the beginning of the chapter. "I AM your free-dom"—is what He told the Jews in the middle of the chapter. "I AM your forever"—is what He tells all of us at the end of the chapter.

There is no Higher Power than Me, there is no higher power than Mine. I AM who I AM, for I AM God. So declares Jesus Christ to your waiting heart and life!

So what are you waiting for?

Several months ago I found myself, late one evening, in a home with two friends and colleagues. We had gathered on behalf of a young man in our midst who was caught in the choking grip of an intense spiritual battle. It was as if the forces of darkness were throt-tling his life and body and with superhuman strength struggling to prevent the young man's freedom.

By his own confession, the man described habits and a lifestyle that had enslaved him and bound him cap-tive. I have never before in my life witnessed such an intense struggle—a battle between the forces of light and the forces of darkness. The physical manifestations made it clear that supernatural forces were struggling for mastery over the young man's life.

But there in that upper room while we prayed, the young man made a decision to embrace the I AM who through His crimson victory on the cross has shattered the dominion and broken the power of darkness. And I witnessed a body and mind and soul set free by the triumphant death of Jesus, the great I AM.

And once again it was proven true, the apocalyptic promise that this same John of the Gospel would write near the end of his life, "They have conquered [the devil] by the blood of the Lamb" (Revelation 12:11).

THE CLAIM

For the only full and forever kind of freedom in the world comes through "the blood of the Lamb," the conquering and triumphant death of Jesus on Calvary. This is the final step.

You see, there isn't a twelve-stepper alive who would deny the horrendous battle that takes place in the human mind and body when a life is struggling to be set free! But it is the final step that brings the battling heart face to face with the only One who can promise a forever kind of victory. The One who declared, " 'If the Son makes you free, you will be free indeed,' " is the same Jesus Christ who "shared in [our] humanity so that by his death he might destroy him who holds the power of death—that is, the devil—and free those who all their lives were held in slavery" (Hebrews 2:14, 15, NIV).

Freedom in the final step. Freedom for the next step in your "one life to live." All you have to do is reach out to this same Jesus with the quiet prayer: "Jesus, save me and set me free—I've given up trying to free myself—I need Your higher power—I need Your forgiving and forever freedom—Jesus, great I AM, I call on You—please set me free."

"And Jesus said [to the woman caught in adultery], 'Neither do I condemn you. Go your way, and from now on do not sin again [i.e., live in bondage to that sin anymore].' " " '[For] if the Son makes you free, you will be free indeed' " (John 8:11, 36).

CHAPTER
4

"Guiding Light"
I AM the light of the world

Did you think of the same thing I did when you saw the live videocam pictures? I thought of the fiery Apocalypse!

Who will ever forget the live news shots from the hovering helicopter swirling above the windswept brow of that posh Malibu villa? The Spanish stucco mansion appeared as if it were descending into a lake of fire. Perhaps you saw that bit of news clip, one more piece of footage in reporting what seemed to be the interminable hillside fires of southern California a few months ago.

The Malibu estate in this particular clip was actually not on fire. The newscam's telephoto lens, however, created the surreal appearance of an entire sky of roaring and raging orange—whipped into the fury of hell by the Santa Ana winds that rushed their flames up the bone-dry hillside toward the crystalline white walls of that helpless mansion.

It looked like the wall of flame was only inches from the walls of stucco. Down below the helicopter, the residents of the villa were racing back and forth across the lawn. One man had climbed up onto an outcropping beside the mansion. He stood there all alone and watched—silhouetted against the orange river of flame.

THE CLAIM

And when the night fell, the serpentine river of orange flame flowed on through the darkness.

Could it be that what we witnessed on the evening news was a metaphor, a portent of an entire planet on fire? (And did you notice—nobody could put the fire out? It only stopped when the winds ceased.) One ancient writer described the metaphor in this way, "The day of the Lord will come like a thief, and then the heavens will pass away with a loud noise, and the elements will be dissolved with fire" (2 Peter 3:10).

I have heard well-known pulpiteers across our country decry the litany of natural disasters we've been experiencing of late—fires and floods and hurricanes and quakes—as judgments of God upon our nation. But are they right? Shall we blame God for the natural tragedies that randomly stalk our land? Or could it be that we live in a civilization that is caught in the deadly cross-fire of evil forces that would destroy us all? Maybe the fire fall in this benighted hour of history isn't God at all. Maybe behind the shadows that cloak us are the arrayed powers of darkness that seek our destruction in this night.

But the more urgent question is, In this dark and thick night of civilization, is there is a light to guide us, to save us? A "guiding light" to shine on our night-enshrouded paths and lead us through our starless shadows into eternal day?

In yet another radical I AM claim, Jesus answers Yes to our query. Yes, there is a guiding Light. Find this Light, and you will never be lost or left in the night again.

"As he walked along, [Jesus] saw a man blind from birth" (John 9:1). What you are about to read is one of the most amazing miracles recorded anywhere in the Gospels. Not only is this the only miracle in the four

Gospels involving a physical malady that has existed from birth; it is also a dramatic healing that blends a pair of blind eyes, a muddy glob of spit, and an explosive confrontation with the religious hierarchy of the day into a shining portrayal of the "guiding light."

The man had been born blind. The disciples of Jesus knew it, and they were more than curious. "His disciples asked him, 'Rabbi, who sinned, this man or his parents, that he was born blind?' " (verse 2).

You see, the Jews taught that the sufferings of this life were a divine punishment for sin. (Which sounds a lot like the national preachers we noted above.) In their religious book, the Talmud, there appeared statements like this: "There is no death without sin, and there is no suffering without iniquity." Or "A sick man does not recover from his sickness until all his sins are forgiven him."

Furthermore, the rabbis taught that God was careful to match each sin with its peculiar form of punishment. In fact, they believed that in some cases it was possible to determine the guilt of the individual by the nature of his suffering!

So who sinned? the disciples wondered out loud to Jesus.

"Jesus answered, 'Neither this man nor his parents sinned; he was born blind so that God's works might be revealed in him [The original language can also be translated here, "But as a result of his being born blind, God's works will be revealed and made manifest now."]' " (verse 3).

But Jesus isn't through. As a prelude to this dramatic miracle, He makes a radical claim that will be proven by the healing: " 'We must work the works of him who sent me while it is day; night is coming when no one can work. As long as I am in the world, *I AM the light of*

THE CLAIM

the world' " (verses 4, 5, emphasis supplied).

What does that radical I AM claim mean? Finish the story. Because the very next sound you hear is the deep, guttural rumbling of someone preparing to clear his throat in expectoration! Which, of course, is a polite and sanitized description for spit.

My wife Karen dislikes watching baseball games for that reason. She claims that baseball players are forever spitting and spitting and spitting throughout the game. While some of us may tolerate expectorating on the ball field, most of us are pretty settled on forbidding the act elsewhere in our socially clean and sterile world.

But the ancients ascribed great medicinal properties to human spit. And so in deference to that "old husband's" tale, Jesus uses His own spit on three separate occasions in the Gospels to perform a healing. Which is why you can hear Him clear His throat in this story and spit on the ground and pick up that muddy clump of dirt and mix it around in His palm and then gently smear it onto the sightless sockets of this blind man.

The man can feel the warm, gritty mud being spread over his lightless eyes. Then Jesus speaks, " 'Go, wash in the pool of Siloam' " (verse 7).

You can picture the blind man, can't you? His eyes smeared with brown and dripping mud, he stumbles down the crowded alleyway, crying out for someone to point him in the direction of Siloam. His heart pounding, he gropes as fast as his tripping feet will let him in the direction he's been pointed.

Finally arriving at Siloam, he inches his way gingerly to the edge of the pool. He cautiously crouches down on his knees and hesitatingly stoops over to thrust his hands deep into the cool waters.

Once, twice, maybe three times for good measure, he splashes the water across his crusted sockets until he can feel that the spit and dirt are gone. Do you think he's scared to try opening his eyes? (Maybe he had been born with no sockets at all!)

But never mind, for one thing is certain: When that man opened his eyes and the rainbow of sunlight filtered through the water that still clung to his eyelids, you could hear him shouting a mile away! And he "came home seeing" (verse 7, NIV). Because when Jesus gets ahold of you, you always come home seeing.

But of course, the neighbors aren't privy to that bit of truth. And the buzz of their confusion is heard up and down the street. " 'Is this not the man who used to sit and beg?' Some were saying, 'It is he.' Others were saying, 'No, but it is someone like him.' He kept saying, 'I am the man.' But they kept asking him, 'Then how were your eyes opened?' He answered, 'The man called Jesus made mud, spread it on my eyes, and said to me, "Go to Siloam and wash." Then I went and washed and received my sight' " (verses 8-11).

Now everybody's in a state of confusion! Looks like they'll have to take this matter up with the ecclesiastical tribunal down the street. So off the neighbors go, hauling their newly sighted friend with them.

"Now it was a sabbath day when Jesus made the mud and opened his eyes" (verse 14). And that made it very bad news for the Pharisees. Because not only did they intensely dislike this popular young teacher named Jesus; they found it particularly onerous that He would dare to perform such a dramatic healing on the Sabbath. After all, had not the religious hierarchy instituted a massive codification of Sabbath laws designed to enforce Sabbath observance? And didn't their exacting code make this Jesus a Sabbath breaker?

THE CLAIM

The healed man is arraigned before the tribunal, and the cross-examination begins. Once they ascertain that it is indeed the same Jesus they know who performed this healing, they exclaim in the hearing of all, " 'This man [Jesus] is not from God, for he does not observe the sabbath' " (verse 16.) Then turning to the former blind man, they probe him, " 'What do you say about him? It was your eyes he opened' " (verse 17).

And the healed man quickly retorts that his healer must surely be a prophet. Which, of course, only inflames the leaders!

Attempting to squelch the blind man's testimony, they quickly summon his parents to the tribunal. Maybe his mother and father will shed some light on this conundrum. But they don't. Because when the Pharisees ask how their son has been miraculously healed, the parents aren't willing to risk excommunication from the synagogue by affirming faith in this Jesus, so they lamely pass the buck back to their boy: " 'Ask him; he is of age' " (verse 21).

So the Pharisees do. And in a circus of confusion they charge Jesus with being a sinner and end up eliciting a beautiful confession from the healed man: " 'I do not know whether [this Jesus] is a sinner. One thing I do know, that though I was blind, now I see' " (verse 25).

The prelates are now furious! What was supposed to have been a public condemnation of the young Preacher is turning into a compelling testimony in His defense! Furiously, they cross-examine the healed man all over again. And he is just as nonplussed: " 'I have told you already, and you would not listen. Why do you want to hear it again? Do you also want to become his disciples?' " (verse 27).

Wrong! The ecclesiastics now explode with invectives against this undaunted once-blind man. When their reviling has abated for a moment, the healed man calmly, in a masterful display of irrefutable logic, nails the clerics to their own theological wall: " 'Here is an astonishing thing! . . . We know that God does not listen to sinners, but he does listen to one who worships him and obeys his will. Never since the world began has it been heard that anyone opened the eyes of a person born blind. If this man were not from God, he could do nothing' " (verses 30-33).

But in the face of such convincing logic, the infuriated Pharisees "drove him out" (verse 34).

The story ends with a question mark, doesn't it? Because which of the characters really was the most blind?

The headline caught my eye. It was a quotation from Jody Powell, press secretary for former president Jimmy Carter. There he was on the front page, giving a speech for the Sinai Sunday Evening Forum down in Michigan City, Indiana, a few years ago.

And the headline read, "Powell: Lies necessary sometimes."

The story went on to quote him as saying: "Government officials have the right to deceive the American people."

They do?

Powell hastened to explain that he didn't mean for political or personal reasons but only in the cases of national interest.

And then he went on to tell how he lied to the press during the Iranian hostage crisis. When asked by a *Los Angeles Times* reporter if the administration was planning to rescue the hostages, Powell confessed to his Michigan City audience: "I lied. Not only did I lie, but I told the most convincing and elaborate lie that I could come up with." He went on, "There are those occasions [of national security] in which government officials do have the right to deceive or lie to or mislead the press and, therefore, the people that they were elected or appointed to serve."

Is he right? If he is, then you're going to be hard pressed to explain the difference between national security and personal security! Why else do people bend the truth, which is a euphemism for lying? Why do people cheat and steal? Simply because they figure that their own private national security is at stake. "I'll lose or get fired or not be liked if I don't! So if it's right for you to lie, Jody Powell, it's right for me to lie too."

After all, everybody does it, right? Charles Schultz described the utter pervasiveness of dishonesty in society today through one of his "Peanuts" cartoon strips. Lucy and Linus are chatting, when Charlie Brown walks by. Linus turns to Lucy: "One thing I have to admit about Charlie Brown—he is absolutely without guile." To which Lucy replies as she stares after Charlie Brown: "I knew he was missing something."

Because anymore if you find a man or a woman without guile and without dishonesty, society concludes there must be something wrong with that poor soul— "I knew he was missing something."

Rudolph Giuliani, the newly elected mayor of New York City, while U.S. attorney for the city, conducted a "sting" operation that swept from Long Island to the Canadian border. As part of the operation, an undercover FBI agent posed as a salesman of steel products. Quoting Giuliani now, "On 106 occasions, bribes were offered or discussed. On 105 of those occasions, the public official involved accepted the bribe. And on the other occasion he didn't think the amount was enough." The headline to the story read "N.Y. 'sting' finds no honest man."

So how many honest men and women are there anymore?

After all, television lies, the media lie, Hollywood lies, lawyers lie, students lie, marriage partners lie, businesspeople lie, even politicians lie. Which makes about everybody, right? That was the tongue-in-cheek insinuation of a *Time* magazine cover story, "Lying— Everybody's Doin' It (Honest)" (5 October 1992).

But before we all exclaim—"Whew! Thank God, I'm not a politician or any of those other liars!"—perhaps we'd do well to inquire about our own lives around the home or school or even church.

Jeff JanVonderen, in his book *Tired of Trying to Measure Up*, lists a few lines you may have heard once or twice in your life too. They illustrate what he calls the "can't win" rule, which "is really two contradictory rules combined into one":

> • Always tell the truth; but when we go to Grandma's, don't tell her you hate her bread stuffing. If she asks, just be polite, eat it, and say you like it.
> Or,
> • Honesty is the best policy; but, if so-and-so calls, tell them I'm not here.
> Or,
> • Don't keep anything from your parents; but Mother (or Father) would be so upset if they knew this, so please don't tell them (43).

We've all lived with some of that childhood dissonance, haven't we? Nobody intentionally set out to distort the truth or tell a lie. It's just that it comes so easily for us.

And it isn't always a matter of telling a lie either.

THE CLAIM

Sometimes we unconsciously end up living by a lie. JanVonderen, a pastoral psychologist, goes on to list some of the lies we live by:

- What's *real* doesn't matter; how things *look* is what matters.
- What other people think is most important.
- Feelings don't matter.
- If parents are upset, the behavior of their kids is the cause.
- If parents are upset, the behavior of the kids is the solution.
- There's a different set of ethical and moral rules for adults than there is for kids.
- If you can't say something nice, don't say anything at all.
- We can solve all of our problems ourselves.
- We don't have any problems.
- Peace at all costs (ibid., 44).

The fact is, we all struggle over living with a lie. And whether you twist the truth or tell a lie, what difference does it make? It always leaves you blinded to reality in the end and lost in the dark of your own dishonesty. Which makes us no better than the man who was born blind, now, does it?

So is there any hope for us who were born blind, the ones M. Scott Peck calls "the people of the lie"?

Yes! exclaims this radical claim of Jesus. For our darkness there is hope. "Again Jesus spoke to them, saying, 'I AM the light of the world. Whoever follows me will never [another double negative in the original language, "no not"] walk in darkness but will have the light of life' " (John 8:12).

There it is, the healing truth for our blindness—to

forsake the dark, we must follow the Light. And " 'I AM the light of the world.' "

It must be noted that the One who declared, "I AM the light *of* the world," was the same One who commanded, " 'Let there be light' " *in* the world (Genesis 1:3). The Jesus of John was the Creator God of Genesis. John himself is unequivocal in affirming that truth:

> In the beginning was the Word, and the Word was with God, and the Word was God. He was in the beginning with God. All things came into being through him, and without him not one thing came into being. . . . And the Word became flesh and lived among us (John 1:1-3, 14).

Which simply means that the One who healed the blind man on the Sabbath was Himself the Lord of the Sabbath (see Matthew 12:8).

It was He who gave the seventh-day Sabbath as a shining gift of time and friendship to Adam and Eve in the Garden of Eden (see Genesis 2:1-3).

It was He, the great I AM, who with His own finger carved the majestic words of the fourth commandment in the Decalogue as a perpetual reminder to all generations:

> Remember the Sabbath day by keeping it holy. Six days you shall labor and do all your work, but the seventh day is a Sabbath to the Lord your God. On it you shall not do any work, neither you, nor your son or daughter, nor your manservant or maidservant, nor your animals, nor the alien within your gates. For in six days the Lord made the heavens and the earth, the sea, and all that is in them, but he rested on

the seventh day. Therefore the Lord blessed the Sabbath day and made it holy (Exodus 20:8-11, NIV).

And when He became Emmanuel—or "God is with us" (Matthew 1:23)—it was He who consistently observed the seventh-day Sabbath throughout His life on earth (see Luke 4:16). Thus it was that He called Himself the Lord of the Sabbath, the One who instituted the Sabbath as God and observed it as Man (see Mark 2:28). Why, even in death, when as the Lord of the Sabbath He became the Lord of salvation, Jesus rested in the grave "according to the commandment" (Luke 23:56). No wonder His disciples did likewise. For even after He ascended to heaven, the New Testament record shows them worshiping the Lord of the Sabbath on the seventh-day Sabbath (see Acts 13:14-16, 42, 44; 16:12, 13; 17:2; 18:1-4).

And when the portrait is painted of God's children throughout eternity, it shows them joyfully worshiping their Creator on the seventh-day Sabbath (see Isaiah 66:22, 23).

Thus, like a golden thread that is woven from Genesis through to Revelation, the divine gift of the seventh-day Sabbath shines in all its God-given luster.

And so when Jesus declared, "I AM the light of the world," just before His Sabbath-day healing of the blind man, He was revealing the inseparable bond between the seventh-day Sabbath and the Light of the world. For in Jesus they are one!

Which means that to follow the Light of the world is to worship the Lord of the Sabbath. " 'I AM the light of the world. Whoever follows me will never walk in darkness but will have the light of life' " (John 8:12). The consistent record of Scripture and the radical claim of

Christ are an irrefutable summons to us today to follow Him who is both the Light of the world and the Lord of the Sabbath.

To do any other is to walk in darkness, is it not? And wouldn't that be the ultimate blindness? For when I decide I don't need His Sabbath, I am declaring I don't want His light. For how can one choose to embrace the Light of the world and at the same time reject the Lord of the Sabbath? That would be living a lie, and that would mean walking in darkness, wouldn't it?

So how, then, shall we be healed, we who have lived in the night of our own blindness? The answer is simple but clear: Follow the Light!

It is no coincidence that when Jesus died on the cross, there was a mysterious darkness that settled like night over Calvary. "When it was noon, darkness came over the whole land until three in the afternoon" (Mark 15:33). It was as if the hellish darkness of every lie we have lived and every commandment we have broken and every sin you and I have ever committed was draped like a black funereal pall over His heart. The starless night of our own lost guilt became His. "And the Lord has laid on him the iniquity of us all" (Isaiah 53:6).

But there in that moment of eternal darkness, another miracle took place and another healing was birthed. For on that center cross, He who is the Light died in the dark so that we in the dark might live in the Light. Gone the lie, gone the night, gone the guilt, gone our sins—for "by his wounds we are healed" (Isaiah 53:5, NIV).

" 'I AM the light of the world. Whoever follows me will never walk in darkness but will have the light of life.' "

So doesn't it make all the sense in the world to follow the Light of the world? "If we say that we have fellowship with him while we are walking in darkness, we lie and do not do what is true; but if we walk in the light as he himself is in the light, we have fellowship with one another, and the blood of Jesus his Son cleanses us from all sin" (1 John 1:6, 7).

In a darkened world lost in its own nightfall, it is time to follow the guiding Light. "I AM the light of the world." And that's good news for every day of the week, including His seventh-day Sabbath!

CHAPTER
5

"Edge of Night"
I AM the door

Does it strike you, too, that we are living in a society where violence is now epidemic, where fear is no longer endemic—it is universal? For us, "Edge of Night" is no longer a fictional soap opera; it has become the razor-sharp edge of fear upon which we all live!

I climbed onto the Metro subway a few weeks ago in the nation's capital for a twenty-minute ride. But with everything I've heard about Washington, D.C., being the "murder capital of America," I'll be right up front and admit to being a bit nervous and jumpy about the prospects of this subterranean ride.

Have you noticed on subways that nobody stares very long at another passenger? It must be an unwritten rule that all passengers must keep to themselves ("and don't bug me").

So when a man boarded our car and began to loudly shout at some of the other occupants on the train, I got really nervous! I was grateful that my stop arrived shortly thereafter.

Why? Because of all I've read and seen and heard about the rising crime wave in our nation's cities, that's why! Cities and a nation on the "edge of night."

Look what Americans read about day after day. Scan the following snatches of news releases, and see for yourself why most of us have concluded that violence is now epidemic in our nation and fear is universal. We all live on the edge of night, the razor's edge of fear, don't we?

According to the experts, murder was the leading cause of workplace death for women in the 1980s and the third leading cause of on-the-job death for all workers. The statistics calculate an average of fifteen workers a week slain on the job during the 1980s! Taxicab drivers were most at risk. And if you're a male, the on-the-job homicide rate is three times that for females! What ever happened to job "security"?

No wonder Deborah Prothrow-Stith wrote the following in an op-ed piece that appeared in the *Chicago Tribune*:

> The problem of violence in America is unlike that in any other developed country. We have a homicide rate for young men that is four times higher than the next most violent country in the world, Scotland, and a rate 70 times that of Austria. The FBI estimates that 1.8 million Americans are victims of violence each year, and that number excludes most family violence. Each month about 420 children die from gunshot injuries. . . . Each year we spend about $64 billion paying for the costs associated with violence. *Each day we become more fearful of violence* (28 December 1993, emphasis supplied).

And it's killing our kids! On January 6, 1994, the National School Boards Association released a survey of our nation's school districts. The NSBA's conclusion? American schools are facing an " 'epidemic of violence' "! Fully 82 percent of the 729 school districts responding to the survey reported an upsurge in violence during the last five years. Sixty-one percent reported weapons incidents. Thirty-nine percent stated that there had been a knifing or shooting in one of their schools. Twenty-three percent reported drive-by shootings. And 15 percent reported at least one rape. Is it any surprise that 78 percent reported student assaults on students, with 60 percent indicating student assaults on teachers? Metal detectors and drug-sniffing dogs have now become a part of the curriculum of many American teenagers.

Nor are college and university campuses exempt from this epidemic of violence. In Michigan alone, campus police reports indicate that during 1992 at least 14,960 crimes were committed on the state's fifteen public university campuses. Are the statistics any different in other states?

But then, should we be surprised with the mounting, alarming evidence that our young people are in trouble? Look at the world they live in; look at the homes they come from. Neil Howe and Bill Strauss have undertaken a sociological analysis of our nation's "baby busters," the youth born since 1961. Their book, *13th Gen*, describes the statistical horror story that these young people are living every twenty-four hours. Across America each day:

- More than 2,500 children witness the divorce or separation of their parents.
- About 90 are taken from their parents' custody and committed to foster homes.
- Some 1,000 unwed teenage girls become mothers.
- Of 15- to 24-year-olds, 13 commit suicide, and 16 are murdered.

THE CLAIM

- Some 500 adolescents begin using illegal drugs, and 1,000 begin drinking alcohol.
- At least 3,610 teenagers are assaulted, 630 are robbed, and 80 are raped.
- More than 100,000 high-school students bring guns to school.
- At least 2,200 teens drop out of high school.
- The typical 14-year-old watches three hours of TV, but does only one hour of homework (page 33).

And all of that happens to our youth every twenty-four hours all year long!

So whom shall we blame? How about television? Brandon Centerwall, an epidemiologist at the University of Washington, has discovered an intriguing piece of statistical evidence. Between 1945 and 1974, the homicide rate in the United States rose by 93 percent. But strangely enough, during the same period in South Africa, homicides among whites declined by 7 percent! How can such disparity be explained? One crucial difference between our two societies during this period was that until 1975, South Africa banned television! Centerwall's conclusion? "Television is not just a showcase for violent behavior but a cause of it."

What's going on! You can't tell me that the bloody and explosive headlines that have become standard fare during our supper-hour newscasts (not to mention the horrific depictions of brutal violence by the entertainment industry) are simply the result of the natural ebb and flow of evolutionary development. It is more than painfully clear that human society and civilization are being catapulted toward self-destruction. For in the history of humankind, there never has been such an escalation of horror and violence.

America has become a nation paralyzed by fear. All the security systems in the world can't seem to halt the bloody rise in urban and rural violence. No presidential commission or congressional bill can staunch the hemorrhaging. If Americans weren't so bent on appearing to have all the answers and to always be in control, we would likely conclude that some sinister mastermind is behind this deadly upsurge in violent, hellish crime!

Take nineteen-year-old James Buquet, who wrote a narrative for his creative-writing class at Grossmont College in San Diego. It was a bizarre piece of writing, but the three students in his study group, to whom he read his paper, didn't think too much about it. After all, "Stephen King writes weird stuff," fellow student Mike Wells would later comment.

What James Buquet wrote in chilling detail was the story of a man named Natas A. Bishop who believed he could give meaning to life by taking it away from others and himself. Buquet described how Natas Bishop methodically prepared for the killings at his home "with the ice of a serial killer going in for the prey."

That was September 15, 1993. On October 14 James Buquet drove to the Family Fitness Center in El Cajon and with a twelve-gauge shotgun killed one man, three women, and finally himself.

The name, again, of the hero in his writing-class story? Natas. Which is *Satan* spelled backward!

Read 1 Peter 5:8 if you want to get a sense for the dark mastermind that is plotting our society's destruction. "Keep alert. Like a roaring lion your adversary the devil prowls around, looking for someone to devour."

There is a destroyer at large, and you already know his name. Spelled backward or forward—he is the same destroyer. And his most potent weapon is fear. For there is no stronger paralysis than fear. Why else do you think fear is so epidemic in this twilight of the twentieth century on the edge of night?

Even you and I, in the tranquil obscurity of our private lives, are paralyzed by our private fears, are we not? We all have them, those moments of quiet desperation when our souls seem threatened with the numinous sense of a fear that will not let go.

For you, it may be the fear of depression, the awful dark fear that somehow your life is simply out of control and nobody can be found to make sense out of it anymore. A shadowy and empty sense of meaninglessness that sucks the emotions into a black hole of despair. Is it the icy clutch of the fear of depression that paralyzes you?

Or it may be the fear of defeat, a sense of failure, that you are of less worth than the others in your class or office or profession "who are obviously more successful than I." Afraid to dare, afraid to try, afraid to risk. Could it be that the fear of defeat has you in its icy clutches?

It could be the fear of divorce that twists your self-worth and shreds your dignity with the crushing thought, "I've been rejected or abandoned or cast off as less than desirable, so my life is worth nothing anymore." Shattered by the tragedy of rejection and failure and paralyzed by the notion that there can be no life after divorce—that icy fear is no stranger to the hearts and homes of America, is it?

What about the fear of disease? Is that what clutches you today? Is it the strangulating anxiety that all the medical intervention in the world isn't going to save your life now, and you will be crushed by a pain, a cancer, a disease that cannot be extinguished? Society's urgent efforts to halt the advance of AIDS and cancer and heart disease are of little comfort if they aren't in time to save the likes of you and me.

But then what is the fear of disease, if in the end it is not the fear that haunts all our naked souls—the fear of death, the most natural and most numinous of all our fears? Who is stranger to that suffocating worry we try to keep pushed into the dark recesses of our minds? That fear of running out of life before we run out of ideas or hopes or loves or dreams or children or grandchildren. The fear of dying before we're ready to go.

No matter which fear is your fear, what John Harris describes is right for all of us:

> Fear is the great destructive force in us. Fear shuts down spontaneity, and most importantly turns us away from others and in upon ourselves. Fear drowns out our capacities for life. . . . Fear makes us afraid of life itself, afraid of the intensity living brings with it. If fear persists in us long enough, we often come to a terrible moment of recognition, perhaps in middle life or later, that life has passed us by, *that we have never really lived the life given to us* (*Stress, Power, and Ministry*, 33, emphasis supplied).

It would be a "terrible moment of recognition," wouldn't it, to wake up one morning and discover that "life has passed us by, that we have never really lived the life given to us"?

So the question for us all is, How can we banish our paralyzing fears and be set free from our crippling insecurities? Is there life beyond the "edge of night"?

Listen to one line from the Gospel of John that today can become for you a revolutionary offer of freedom from fear! Jesus spoke the words, " 'I AM the door; anyone who comes into the fold through me will be safe' " (John 10:9, Revised English Bible). There it is, the fifth radical claim of Christ in John, a word of hope for all who live on the edge of night.

" 'I AM the door; anyone who comes into the fold through me will be safe.' "

Read the verses clustered around this radical claim, and it will quickly be clear to you that Jesus is describing a shepherd with his sheep and his sheepfold.

To better understand Jesus' declaration, it is important to note that shepherds in the time of Christ had two kinds of sheepfolds. They could have a sheepfold beside their house, where they constructed a wall adjacent to their little home and created a small corral-like fold with a door or gate in it.

Or shepherds were known to construct open-air sheepfolds out in the wilds, with makeshift walls and an opening in one of the walls for a door or gate. Particularly with the open-field folds, it was not unusual for the shepherd to gather all his flock into the fold at nightfall and then lie across the open entry and literally become the door of the sheep! By choosing that strategic position to sleep through the night, the shepherd's body actually became a barrier to all intruders, whether thieves or wild beasts. Because nobody could get at the sheep without going over the shepherd's body first. His body became the door to the sheep!

" 'I AM the door; anyone who comes into the fold through me will be safe.' "

The point of Jesus' radical claim is unmistakable. Someone else also stretched out His body to defend His sheep. And when He did, they nailed Him to a cross.

74

But all the blasting and bloody fury of hell could not batter down that crimson Door of safety and salvation!

" 'I AM the door; anyone who comes into the fold through me will be safe.' "

There it is—the antidote for your fears, the answer to your insecurities. And it's all wrapped up in some very good news! You *can* stand up to your fears; you don't have to be victimized any longer. The secret is to stand behind the Door.

Why, you and I learned that lesson when we were kids! Because whenever it's dark outside, parents don't let the children answer the door. Oh, sure, the child may go scampering to the door when the doorbell rings. But a quick command from Mom or Dad instructs the child to wait behind the door. Let Father or Mother open the door and face whoever might be waiting (or lurking) outside in the shadows. The child's instructions are clear: Stay behind the door.

"I AM the door," Jesus declares. So if you want to stand up to your destroyer, then stand behind the Door and stay behind your Defender. You can face any fear when you face it through Jesus.

May I ask it again, Are you afraid? Is your life held in the icy clutch of some forbidding fear? Then for you and me there is this same Jesus, who stands before our minds' eye with His outstretched and nail-scarred hands. " 'I AM the door; anyone who comes into the fold through me will be safe.' "

Over and over again throughout the Scriptures, Jesus repeats the strong assurance of that promise with His invitation to abandon our fears and come to Him:

> • Do not fear, for I am with you, do not be
> afraid, for I am your God; I will strengthen you,
> I will help you, I will uphold you with my victo-

rious right hand (Isaiah 41:10).

• Do not fear, for I have redeemed you; I have called you by name, you are mine. . . . Do not fear, for I am with you (Isaiah 43:1, 5).

• There is no fear in love, but perfect love casts out fear (1 John 4:18).

• God hath not given us the spirit of fear; but of power, and of love, and of a sound mind (2 Timothy 1:7, KJV).

• Be strong and courageous; do not be frightened or dismayed, for the Lord your God is with you wherever you go (Joshua 1:9).

• When you pass through the waters, I will be with you; and through the rivers, they shall not overwhelm you; when you walk through fire you shall not be burned, and the flame shall not consume you (Isaiah 43:2).

• Do not let your hearts be troubled, and do not let them be afraid (John 14:27).

• I AM the door; anyone who comes into the fold through me will be safe (John 10:9, REB).

The next time you sense the shadow of fear lurking in your edge of night, let your heart go for the Door. In the quiet of your mind, begin to repeat the promises you have just read. Stand behind your Door. Remember that Jesus already conquered your destroyer at Calvary. That is why Satan has no power to clutch your life with his icy fear when you stand behind the Door, when you stay behind your Defender.

Jesus is unequivocally clear in His promise to you: " 'Whoever enters by me will be saved' " (John 10:9). *You are safe in Jesus*. You have His word on it.

So the next time fear comes knocking at your door, just remember who your Door is! And let Him take the edge off of night.

CHAPTER
6

"All My Children"

I AM the good shepherd

How many children are in "All My Children"? That depends on who's speaking. If you mean all the children who love and hate and laugh and cry their way through the popular daytime soap opera by the same name, then only the scriptwriters know for sure how many children "all" really is.

But if those three words, "all My children," are spoken by the Father of humanity, then "all" means every one of us! For God has a very big family. A very big and broken family, actually.

She was a mother of two small children when at the age of twenty-five she caught a chill in December. The chill turned to fever, and on January 5, 1840, Mary Lundie died.

The next year her mother published her daughter's memoirs and included in them one of the twenty-three hymns young Mary had written, this one a children's prayer she had composed for her two toddlers.

> Jesus, tender Shepherd, hear me,
> Bless Thy little lamb tonight;
> Through the darkness be Thou near me;
> Watch my sleep till morning light.

"All My Children"

All this day Thy hand has led me,
And I thank Thee for Thy care.
Thou hast clothed me, warmed and fed me;
Listen to my evening prayer.

But posthumously, this short and touching hymn became more than a composition for Mary Lundie's two children. Before long, it became a good-night prayer for children everywhere, who quietly sang its simple words as they drifted off to sleep. "Jesus, tender Shepherd, hear me, / Bless Thy little lamb tonight."

But come to think of it, hasn't the world known a very similar simple prayer for many centuries longer? A quiet prayer of commitment to the same Shepherd. A prayer not only for the end of a day but a prayer often prayed at the end of a life. "Yea, though I walk through the valley of the shadow of death, I will fear no evil: for thou art with me." How many a weary gray head has lain itself down for the last time upon life's pillow with the words of the old King James Psalm 23 upon the lips.

The Lord is my shepherd; I shall not want. He maketh me to lie down in green pastures: he leadeth me beside the still waters. He restoreth my soul: he leadeth me in the paths of righteousness for his name's sake. Yea, though I walk through the valley of the shadow of death, I will fear no evil: for thou art with me; thy rod and thy staff they comfort me. Thou preparest a table before me in the presence of mine enemies: thou anointest my head with oil; my cup runneth over. Surely goodness and mercy shall follow me all the days of my life: and I will dwell in the house of the Lord for ever.

THE CLAIM

There was something mystical and sacred about that long-ago psalm, wasn't there? Once upon a time, it was very reassuring to know that "the Lord is my shepherd." But then, once upon a time, it seemed that practically all of God's children knew the shepherd's psalm.

But who knows it anymore? After all, the times have changed, haven't they? And an ancient agrarian metaphor no longer speaks to a modern urban society.

It makes you wonder. If Jesus could do it all over again, would He call Himself something other than the Good Shepherd? That, in fact, is His sixth radical claim in the Gospel of John—" 'I AM the good shepherd' " (John 10:11). But maybe today He would declare, I am the good psychotherapist. Maybe today He would tell us, I am the good lawyer. Or, I am the good policeman. But Good Shepherd? Good grief, what's a good shepherd?

" 'I AM the good shepherd. The good shepherd lays down his life for the sheep' " (John 10:11).

Could it be that in a world of fragmented relationships, this ancient metaphor still speaks powerfully to our modern plight? Maybe it really is for "all my children."

In Pioneer Memorial Church, where I pastor, there is a towering stained-glass window high above the back of the balcony. It is a stained-glass portrait of Jesus, the Good Shepherd. Twenty feet high, its translucent colors portray Him with two sheep bleating at His side. But in the crook of His arm, He is tenderly holding a quiet and contented lamb. "Jesus, tender Shepherd, hear me, / Bless Thy little lamb tonight."

A portrait of the Good Shepherd framed in the fragments of a stained-glass window. But what in the world does that have to do with contemporary life?

But then again, maybe that's just it. Could it be that

in our broken-glass pain, we can find healing in this stained-glass portrait for all of us children?

Do you know broken-glass pain? Let me share with you some of the shards of broken pain that some of the parishioners I pastor (which is Latin for "shepherd") have shared with me. You may be no stranger to some of this pain yourself.

Do you know the broken-glass pain of a mother's heart that anguishes over her alcoholic son? One rebel child in the midst of "all my children." But they are hot tears of a desperate love when that mother prays out of a broken-glass heart for her one lost child. And all the "all my children" in the world can never take her boy's place. Maybe you have cried those tears too.

And what about that workaholic father who too late discovers that all that overtime has meant not enough time with his little girl—a grown-up little girl now—who's run away from home?

Then there is the broken-glass pain of a wife who mourns her husband's death—not his physical death but his death to the love they once shared long ago. Married singles, they've become. Do you know that pain?

How about the broken-glass pain of a university student who has left a home that was only a house for too many years and has a difficult time now forming any lasting relationships? If you don't know real love, how can you show it? Do you know the pain of looking like family but not living like family?

Or how about the broken-glass pain of a fiancé who mourns the broken covenant of a pledged love? And all the dreams that have come shattering down. And the embarrassment of having to go on. Have you been there too?

Or how about the broken-glass pain of an unem-

THE CLAIM

ployed husband and father who sobs in my office as he worries over how he can now provide for his wife and only child? Is that broken glass your own?

Have you had to carry the fragments of the broken-glass pain an employee suffers over the sense of rejection and failure that a pink-slipped dismissal notice has brought? Fired! No good! Now where?

The broken-glass pain of breakups and breakdowns, of headaches and heartaches, of dysfunctions and despair of "all my children"—for my village is a microcosm of the world—your world, and mine.

Let's face it. We live in a world where too often the glittering reflection we see is nothing more than the glaring light of another day reflected off the shards of our own broken pain. We all live in the fragmented world of broken-glass pain.

But could it be that for our broken-glass pain there is this stained-glass portrait?

> "I AM the good shepherd. The good shepherd lays down his life for the sheep. The hired hand, who is not the shepherd and does not own the sheep, sees the wolf coming and leaves the sheep and runs away—and the wolf snatches them and scatters them. The hired hand runs away because a hired hand does not care for the sheep. I AM the good shepherd. I know my own and my own know me. . . . And I lay down my life for the sheep" (John 10:11-15).

Did you catch that? " 'The good shepherd lays down his life for the sheep' " (verse 11). But what could that possibly mean? Because—forgive me for being so blunt—doesn't it seem a bit odd and strange to you, too, this notion of a human being dying for an animal?

"All My Children"

British screenwriter and director Duncan Evans started out a lucky man that fateful November 2. That was the day the orange sea of fire swept up the hill to his posh rented cottage in Malibu, California, during the recent devastating firestorms. But Duncan Evans was ahead of the fire and managed to flee his cottage before it became engulfed in flames.

A fortunate man, this film director, whose credits included the movies *Fire With Fire* and *Third-Degree Burn*.

But his good fortune turned to tragedy when he realized that his pet Siamese cat wasn't with him. So he raced back into the burning cottage to find his beloved pet. But he succumbed to the flames, and a day later he died from his burns.

His pet cat? It was later found alive, with only its paws and ears burned.

Think about it, though. As heroic as it was, this act of a human dying in his attempt to save an animal (in this case, his pet)—it just doesn't seem right, does it? I mean, the cost of the sacrifice far exceeded the value of the animal being saved, whether you're a cat lover or not. Didn't it?

I was conducting a graveside service at the Rosehill Cemetery here in our university town when one of those in attendance pointed out to me the nearby gravestone of a university professor. And there I was reminded of the story I'd heard when we moved to this parish over a decade ago.

It was the story of a family out on a wind-swept jetty near St. Joseph, Michigan. Their pet dog fell into the churning waters of Lake Michigan, and the professor instinctively jumped in to save the pet. But tragically, in the process, he drowned.

I stood for a moment beside his gravestone. Another

man who died valiantly trying to save his pet.

But as I reflect on these two deaths, I wonder whether the film director and the university professor would have made such saving efforts had they known the incalculable price they would end up paying in order to save their animals. The cost of the sacrifice far exceeds the value of the animal that was saved, does it not?

Would you give your life for an animal? If you were a Palestinian shepherd, then the answer might well be Yes. Because just like the two brave and compassionate men above, shepherds have been known to lay down their lives for their sheep. " 'The good shepherd lays down his life for the sheep.' "

I read of one such incident regarding a Palestinian shepherd grazing his flock between Tiberius and Tabor in northern Galilee. It was springtime. As the shepherd led his sheep through the pasture land, three Bedouin thieves jumped him in an effort to steal from his flock. But rather than fleeing his attackers, the shepherd stood his ground and fought back with his staff. However, armed with their sharp "khanjars" (daggers), the thieves ended up hacking the shepherd to death. He died among the sheep he was defending.

Well, I want to say Bravo again! But again I must confess that it seems the cost of the sacrifice far exceeded the value of the animals saved, whether you're a sheep lover or not!

So what did Jesus mean when He declared, " 'I AM the good shepherd. The good shepherd lays down his life for the sheep' "? Does He speak of animals, or does He mean "all my children"?

A few weeks later, Christ gave the answer when He spoke the immortal words, " 'No one has greater love than this, to lay down one's life for one's friends. . . . I have called you friends' " (John 15:13, 15). Not a shep-

herd dying for his sheep here but rather, a Friend laying down His life for His friends.

And less than twenty-four hours after He spoke those
words, Jesus was dead on a Roman cross. There and
then, the truth was seen that to lay down one's life is
the supreme gift of undying, unrelenting, unconditional
love!

But the question repeats itself: Didn't the cost of the
sacrifice far exceed the value of what was saved? If you
were Jesus, would *you* die for *you* or for *me*? Probably
not! For who in his right mind would choose to exchange the spotless life of the Eternal One for the
stained, fragmented life of a sinner like you or me?

Which is precisely the Bible's most triumphant point.
The cost of the sacrifice truly far exceeded the value of
that which was saved! Which leaves only one word for
such a disproportionate exchange: *love*. Divine,
self-sacrificing love for "all my children."

"For while we were still weak, at the right time Christ
died for the ungodly [i.e., you and me]. Indeed, rarely
will anyone die for a righteous person—though perhaps
for a good person someone might actually dare to die.
But *God proves his love for us* in that while we still
were sinners Christ died for us" (Romans 5:6-8, emphasis supplied).

In his classic bestseller, *A Shepherd Looks at Psalm
23*, Phillip Keller powerfully portrays the consequence
of the choice God's self-sacrificing love made:

> God looked down upon sorrowing, struggling,
> sinning humanity and was moved with compas-
> sion for the contrary, sheep-like creatures He
> had made. In spite of the tremendous personal
> cost it would entail to Himself to deliver them
> from their dilemma He chose deliberately to

descend and live amongst them that He might deliver them.

This meant laying aside His splendor, His position, His prerogatives as the perfect and faultless One. He knew He would be exposed to terrible privation, to ridicule, to false accusations, to rumor, gossip and malicious charges that branded Him as a glutton, drunkard, friend of sinners and even an imposter. It entailed losing His reputation. It would involve physical suffering, mental anguish and spiritual agony.

In short, His coming to earth as the Christ, as Jesus of Nazareth, was a straightforward case of utter self-sacrifice that culminated in the cross of Calvary. The laid-down life, the poured-out blood were the supreme symbols of total selflessness. This was *love*. This was *God*. This was *divinity* in action, delivering men from their own utter selfishness, their own stupidity, their own suicidal instincts as lost sheep unable to help themselves (107, 108).

" 'The greatest love a person can have for his friends is to give his life for them. . . . I call you friends' " (John 15:13, 15, TEV). There is no greater love!

Good news for our broken-glass pain, because the Friend who laid down His life for us is the Friend who can pick up the pieces for us. His own bloodstained, broken-glass death on Calvary is all the evidence we need to know that He not only experienced the fragmented depths of our own painful shards, but He also earned the right to shepherd our broken lives back into wholeness again! Healing and hope for "all my children."

Do you know what that means? It means there's no

point, my friend, in your bleating and bleeding alone in the night. It's time to let the stained-glass Shepherd heal your broken-glass pain. He calls you His friend; He calls you by name (John 10:3—" 'He calls his own sheep by name' ")! You are more than a sheep to Him; *you are a friend of His!*

So why hold your life back? Why hesitate any longer to give your broken-glass self to Jesus? Tell Him the truth. Share with Him the tears of your hurt and pain, and admit to Him that you've exhausted every dead-ended avenue in trying to heal yourself—only to find your life fragmented worse than before. Open up your heart and life to Jesus *right now*. And ask Him to pick up your pieces and mend your broken heart.

Look what He offers in exchange! " 'I have come in order that you might have life—life in all its fullness' " (John 10:10, TEV). Can you believe it! In exchange for your broken-glass pain, Jesus is offering you "life in all its fullness." What all the tranquilizers and alcohol and money in the world can't give you, Jesus offers with His outstretched, nail-scarred hands, the hands of the Good Shepherd.

> Jesus, tender Shepherd, hear me,
> Bless Thy little lamb tonight;
> Through the darkness be Thou near me;
> Watch my sleep till morning light.

It happened years ago at a grand social function in England. One of the celebrated actors of the land was asked to get up and recite something for the pleasure of the guests that evening.

The actor consented, and as he took his place before the gathering, he asked if perchance anybody present might have a personal selection for him to recite. An elderly man toward the back of the room raised his hand and asked, "Could you, sir, please recite the twenty-third psalm?"

To which the great actor confidently asserted, "Why, of course, I can. And when I am through, I'll invite you, my old friend, to do the same." The elderly man was a bit embarrassed by the proposal but quietly nodded his assent.

Impressively, the skilled actor recited the beloved psalm. His sonorous voice and intonation were without flaw, his cadence measured and grand. And when he was through, the spellbound audience burst into applause.

Then it was that the elderly man was motioned to the podium. Making his way slowly toward the front, he finally stood before the evening guests. And there he began to recite the psalm. His voice was raspy and hardly remarkable, his cadence a bit awkward. And when he finished, there was no applause—only silence. Heads were bowed in reverence. And not a few eyes were moist with tears.

After several moments of silence, the great actor rose to his feet and with great emotion spoke again: "My friends, I have reached your eyes and ears tonight. But this man has touched your hearts." The actor paused. "The difference is clear. I know the twenty-third psalm. But he knows the Shepherd."

Isn't it time that knowing the Good Shepherd became the clear difference in your life too? Your Friend is ready when you are.

CHAPTER 7

"General Hospital"

I AM the resurrection and the life

I don't know about you, but I really don't relish the thought of dying. I don't mean to be irreverent about death or discourteous about dying, but I simply am not attracted to that possibility at this stage in my life. Which doesn't mean, of course, that there aren't those moments in some human creatures' lives when dying becomes a compelling and even attractive alternative to going on living. I have visited with people who feel that way, and I certainly cannot blame them.

Here in my home state of Michigan, Dr. Jack Kevorkian is in the news again. The whole world has come to know "the suicide doctor." And his repeated assisted suicides continue to dramatically remind us all that there really are people alive who would rather not be. The latest gallows humor in Michigan is the circulation of a gift certificate that says, "Good for one free visit to the clinic of Dr. Jack Kevorkian."

But the fact is, death has never been humorous. Television offers a soap-opera treatment of love in the midst of death and dying called "General Hospital." But I must confess that in all the hospitals I visit (and there have been many in my life of pastoring), I have never found general hospitals to be entertaining at all, opera or not!

A few months ago the National Center for Health Statistics released a nationwide mortality survey, and from its compiled conclusions, a very bleak picture of death and dying in the United States emerges. The 250-page study focused on the last year of life for 17,000 of the two million Americans over the age of twenty-four who died in 1986. Including data gathered from hospitals, nursing homes, and other health-care facilities, the researchers interviewed the next of kin or another close relative for each of those in the 17,000 study group.

What did they find? The Associated Press report on their research announced what you and I may have already suspected: The last year of life is often the worst. Half of the 17,000 needed help or special equipment for such simple activities as dressing, walking, and bathing. More than a third needed help with eating. More than a fourth lived alone, and one-sixth had an annual income of less than $5,000—not just for themselves but for their families.

It doesn't exactly make you want to die, does it? In a pointed understatement, Isadore Seeman, the seventy-six-year-old researcher who authored the report, concluded that "there certainly is a strong indication that these are difficult times for people."

Did he say, "Difficult times for people"? But then anybody who knows anything about death and dying and general hospitals would have no quarrel with that conclusion, would he? So who wants to die?

Not you, not I! Although, of course, sequestered in the most secret hiding places of all our hearts lies the truth of the inevitable—we are all *going* to die someday. Some of us will die sooner than others—but we will all die. For we have a rendezvous with death.

Alan Seeger, in one of the greatest pieces of poetry to emerge from the carnage of the First World War, was brutally right, as his own untimely death at twenty-eight on a now-forgotten battlefield proved:

> I have a rendezvous with Death
> At some disputed barricade
> When Spring comes round with rustling shade
> And apple blossoms fill the air.
> I have a rendezvous with Death
> When Spring brings back blue days and fair.
>
> It may be he shall take my hand
> And lead me into his dark land
> And close my eyes and quench my breath;
> It may be I shall pass him still.
> I have a rendezvous with Death
> On some scarred slope of battered hill,
> When Spring comes round again this year
> And the first meadow flowers appear.
>
> God knows 'twere better to be deep
> Pillowed in silk and scented down,
> Where love throbs out in blissful sleep,
> Pulse nigh to pulse, and breath to breath,
> Where hushed awakenings are dear . . .
> But I've a rendezvous with Death
> At midnight in some flaming town,
> When Spring trips north again this year,
> And I to my pledged word am true,
> I shall not fail that rendezvous.*

And so, because we all have a rendezvous with death, it seems the right time to face it and discuss it while we're still very much alive, you and I, and perhaps far

---

*Roy J. Cook, comp. *One Hundred and One Famous Poems* (Chicago: Reilly and Lee Publishers, 1958), 10.

away from the general hospitals of our land. But let us face death, not with the abandoned resignation of Alan Seeger; let us stare death in the face through the radical and revolutionary claim of Jesus Christ—words spoken over the dead body of a very close friend.

"Now a certain man was ill, Lazarus of Bethany, the village of Mary and her sister Martha. . . . So the sisters sent a message to Jesus, 'Lord, he whom you love is ill' " (John 11:1, 3).

Before we take another step into this epic story, I want you to mark those words well: "The one you love is sick" (NIV, verse 3). The friends of Jesus *do* get sick. And they *do* die. We live in a world mad with the obscenities of disease and death. How wonderful it would be if God somehow immunized all His children with a disease-resistant shield that would shelter them from the ravages of death! But, alas, it is not that way in a world still held in the sway of heaven's archenemy!

"The one you love is sick." And so the loved friends of Jesus do get sick and die. Which, I suppose, is a quiet reminder for the day in which you and I get sick and die, a reminder that when that day comes, we are still loved by Jesus. And so if you are sick today or you are dying tonight, you must know that in the midst of your crucible of suffering you are loved by the One who loved Lazarus.

But then, isn't He a bit strange, this friend of Lazarus?

The messenger from Bethany gasps out the urgent summons, and what does Jesus do? He says a word or two about God's glory being what counts and then spends two more days with the masses, away from His dying friend!

Come on! We know the story. Lazarus ends up dying! And where is God? Two days away! But then again, maybe that disconsolate thought will end up being a treasured fragment of good news to all the rest of us who are dying or will one day die and feel just like Lazarus and his two sisters must have felt—two days away from God. Because two days away or an eternity away, look what this same Jesus can do! But then, we're getting ahead of the story.

"After having heard that Lazarus was ill, he stayed two days longer in the place where he was" (verse 6).

Two days may have seemed forever to His friends in Bethany, but it wasn't. Because Jesus finally did come. On a hot and dusty afternoon, Jesus came walking into a village called Bethany. Emmanuel, "God is with us," had arrived (see Matthew 1:23).

"When Jesus arrived, he found that Lazarus had already been in the tomb four days. . . . When Martha heard that Jesus was coming, she went and met him, while Mary stayed at home. Martha said to Jesus, 'Lord, if you had been here, my brother would not have died' " (verses 17, 20, 21).

"Lord, if you had been here!" Oh, how many times have those very words been sobbed—Lord, if You had only been here, my husband, my wife, my son, or my daughter would not have died; my father, my mother, my brother, my sister, my lover, my friend . . . wouldn't have died. If only You had been here, Jesus!

To the heartbroken cries of a death-ridden planet, what can Jesus answer, what does Jesus say?

"Jesus said to her, 'Your brother will rise again.' Martha said to him, 'I know that he will rise again in the resurrection on the last day' " (verses 23, 24). And then Jesus, in the most radical claim He will ever make, gazes into the depths of Martha's red and teary eyes and declares: " 'I AM the resurrection and the life. Those who believe in me, even though they die, will live, and everyone who lives and believes in me will never die.

Do you believe this?' " (verses 25, 26).

Poor, heartbroken Martha. It is more than her grief-benumbed mind can grasp. All she can muster is the quiet confession, " 'Yes, Lord, I believe that you are the Messiah, the Son of God, the one coming into the world' " (verse 27).

Moments later, Mary, her younger sister, is also bowed at the feet of their Master, and she, too, weeps the painful, wishful prayer, " 'Lord, if [only] you had been here' " (verse 32).

But He wasn't there, not in time, anyway. Never mind, though. Jesus will pay His last respects to His friend. And so He asks, " 'Where have you laid him?' " (verse 34). Did they take Him by the hand, these mourning sisters? Or in silence did He quietly follow their tear-splashed pathway to the tomb?

One thing the record is unequivocal about—the heart of Lazarus and Martha and Mary's Friend felt the pain and shared the tears, for "Jesus wept" (verse 35, KJV). It is the shortest verse in all of Scripture, but it is the longest verse in splashing the colors of divine love across the canvass of human grief and tragedy.

"Jesus wept." And He still weeps. William Blake wrote:

> Till our grief is fled and gone
> He doth sit by us and moan.

Brennan Manning put it this way in his book *Lion and Lamb*: "When Jesus wept . . . , the ground of all being shook, the source of all life trembled, the heart of all love burst open, and the unfathomable depth of God's immense, inexhaustible caring revealed itself" (128).

This is the great I AM God who weeps at our bedsides, who grieves at our gravesides. But through His tears—and ours too—He smiles, for He remembers the rest of the story:

> Then Jesus, again greatly disturbed, came to the tomb. It was a cave, and a stone was lying against it. Jesus said, "Take away the stone." Martha, the sister of the dead man, said to him, "Lord, already there is a stench because he has been dead four days." Jesus said to her, "Did I not tell you that if you believed, you would see the glory of God?" So they took away the stone. And Jesus looked upward and said, "Father, I thank you for having heard me. I knew that you always hear me, but I have said this for the sake of the crowd standing here, so that they may believe that you sent me." When he had said this, he cried with a loud voice, "Lazarus, come out!" The dead man came out, his hands and feet bound with strips of cloth, and his face wrapped in a cloth. Jesus said to them, "Unbind him, and let him go" (verses 38-44).

And what shall we learn from this ancient story, we who live in a world of general hospitals from which too many of the ill never leave alive?

Standing with Jesus in front of Lazarus's tomb, we may learn the truth about death, that one inescapable reality that every general hospital and hospice and nursing home in the world lives with. We may learn the incontrovertible truth that death is a sleep!

That's what Jesus Himself taught through this very episode. While they are still two days away from Bethany, Jesus turns to His disciples and tells them, " 'Our friend Lazarus has fallen asleep, but I am going there to awaken him' " (verse 11). And good health advocates that they are, the disciples know—like everybody knows—that if a person is seriously ill, he really does need his sleep! And so immediately they protest to Jesus that they ought to let Lazarus get all the sleep he needs (verse 12).

But in unmistakable language, Jesus explains Himself: He "had been speaking about his death, but they thought that he was referring merely to sleep. Then Jesus told them plainly, 'Lazarus is dead' " (verse 13, 14).

You see, to the One who declares Himself to be the Resurrection and the Life, what is death? It is nothing! It is nothing but a sleep—a quiet cessation of life, an unconscious state where all cognitive and biological processes of life come to a dead stop. "*Lazarus is asleep—Lazarus is dead.*"

When you're dead tired and you fall into bed, the sleep that follows is deep and unconscious—you and I know that well enough from personal experience. And when that heartless alarm clock rudely begins its incessant chanting or beeping or ringing in the early morning—how often have you awakened with no concept of the passage of time? Why? You were—as we often describe it—dead to the world, that's why! "Lazarus is asleep—Lazarus is dead."

And with that clarion declaration Jesus is in perfect agreement with the rest of Holy Scriptures. The "soul" and "spirit" of human beings are referred to over 1,700 times in the Bible *but are never once said to be immortal or eternal*. In fact, the Bible clearly states that only God is immortal (1 Timothy 6:14-16). The spirit that returns to God at death is not a conscious entity, but the breath of life (Ecclesiastes 12:7; Genesis 2:7). The words *spirit*, *wind*, and *breath* in our English translations come from the same original Hebrew and Greek words in the Bible.

The Bible says the dead cannot remember or give thanks (Psalm 6:5), cannot praise God (Psalm 115:17; Isaiah 38:18), cannot think (Psalm 146:3, 4), and cannot function (Ecclesiastes 9:5, 6, 10). Their abode is the grave, not heaven (Acts 2:29, 34).

So when Jesus makes His unequivocal declaration that *"Lazarus is asleep—Lazarus is dead,"* He is in good company with the Bible prophets who over seventy times also describe death as a sleep!

But neither Jesus nor the prophets are alone anymore. Increasingly, well-known scholars are aligning themselves with the Bible teaching regarding the nonimmortality of the soul, or "soul sleep." John R. W. Stott and Oscar Cullman—part of a growing list of luminaries in the theological world—have gone on published record renouncing their former belief in an immortal soul and declaring the Bible teaching about death as an unconscious cessation of life.

Otherwise, why have a resurrection at all? Jesus' and the Bible teaching about resurrection would be utterly absurd and illogical, would it not, were it true that when a person dies he or she doesn't really die? If that were the case, what would be the point of Jesus going through the motions of purporting a resurrection for Lazarus in the first place? If Lazarus had already been in heaven, why did Jesus *raise him from the dead?* And why did Jesus bother claiming to be "the resurrection and the life," if it were true that when you die, you immediately wing your way to another level or form of life?

The truth is that what most Christians have been taught and what most world religions still teach about death simply cannot be supported by the biblical evidence.

Take, for example, two national bestsellers—two

books that in their unique way end up denying the advance of death through their intelligent but tragically misinformed twist on life. Both books offer the highly touted philosophy that life never ends, even at death—it just keeps going on and on. It is the philosophy of the New Age movement, a growing global movement that claims both authors as its own.

First, there is the national bestseller by Marianne Williamson, *A Return to Love: Reflections on the Principles of "A Course in Miracles."* One of my parishioners is a nurse at a nearby hospital. She dropped the book by with a note that not only is the book a national bestseller—it was proving to be very popular among her colleagues as it made the rounds at the hospital. So I read it, and true to New Age form were these words I came across:

> "There is no death. The Son of God is free."
> *A Course in Miracles* [the New Age compendium upon which Williamson's book is a commentary] says that birth is not a beginning but a continuation, and death is not an end but a continuation. Life goes on forever. It always was and always will be. Physical incarnation is just one form that life can take (262).

There it is, the trademark identification of New Age philosophy regarding death—there is no death! Life just goes on and on and on. Reincarnation, they call it.

To illustrate the "reality" of such reincarnation, Williamson utilizes a clever analogy:

> Physical incarnation is a classroom experience, and souls come to the class to learn what they need to learn. It's much like tuning in to a

channel [*channel* is a word New Age advocates often use to describe contact with the unseen world of "human spirits"] on a television. Let's say we're all tuned to Channel 4. When someone dies, they're no longer on Channel 4, but that doesn't mean they're not broadcasting. They're now on Channel 7 or 8 (263).

And with that depiction, Williamson goes on to suggest that people have actually reported "seeing a light exiting through the top of the head of a dying person" (ibid.). And all this in a national bestseller consumed by American readers! Are we believers too?

Thumb through the book, and you will read assertions such as: "There's actually no place where God stops and you start" (31); "focus on Christ means focus on the goodness and power that lie latent within us" (33); and "Jesus and other enlightened masters are our evolutionary elder brothers" (42).

Where did Williamson and her source volume, *A Course in Miracles*, possibly come up with such notions? On the next-to-the-last page of her bestseller is this revealing statement: " *'Do not make the pathetic error of "clinging to the old rugged cross." The only message of crucifixion is that you can overcome the cross'* " (Williamson's emphasis). Who in the cosmos of our human existence do you suppose would suggest that it is a "pathetic error" to "cling to the old rugged cross"? Could it be the very one whose kingdom was shattered by the cross of Jesus long ago (see John 12:31-33)?

In all fairness, it must be noted that the New Age movement actually is an intellectual effort, a quest by hundreds of thousands of Americans to meet the gnawing hunger in our nation today for spiritual revival.

THE CLAIM

Duncan S. Foster has edited a careful assessment of the New Age movement in his book *New Age Spirituality*. Anyone who reads the literature from this movement comes away realizing that much of what it espouses springs from a deep hunger to love the world meaningfully and to make a better home out of this chaotic planet. So there is genuine good that can be gleaned from New Age philosophy and teaching. The danger is in its subtle mixing of good with error.

Take the second national bestseller, a new book by the bestselling author M. Scott Peck, *Further Along the Road Less Traveled*. It is a sequel to his five-million-copy bestseller *The Road Less Traveled*. Work your way through the sequel, and you will, as I did, marvel over the depth of insight and psychiatric wisdom that Peck dispenses. And by the millions, readers have turned to his writings, in twenty languages, for help and counsel and inspiration.

But when it comes to the theme of death, what does this eminent psychiatrist turned quasi philosopher and lay theologian conclude?

> While open to the possibility of reincarnation, I perhaps would be more passionate about it were there not an alternative way of dealing with the issue, which has come to appeal to me much more deeply—namely, the traditional Christian belief in life after death with its concepts of Heaven, Hell, and Purgatory. . . . On the other hand, I find distasteful the traditional idea of Christianity which preaches the resurrection of the body. Frankly, I see my body as more of a limitation than a virtue, and I will be glad to be free of it rather than having to continue to cart it around. *I prefer to believe that*

souls can exist independently from bodies and
even to be developed independently of bodies
(169, emphasis supplied).

Of course, this psychiatrist is entitled to his opin-
ion—we all have the right to espouse whatever we
choose to believe. But to the millions who haven't
thought through the implications of Peck's opinions and
the underlying theses of the New Age movement, how
globally influential these words suddenly become!

Let me be very blunt in wondering—could it be that
in meeting the deep longing of readers for spiritual revival, these two books—and scores of others like them—
very innocently but very effectively echo the
fork-tongued primeval lie of the serpent to Eve in the
garden, when he hissed, " 'You will not die . . . you will
be like God' " (Genesis 3:4, 5)? Shall we believe "that
ancient serpent, who is called the Devil and Satan, the
deceiver of the whole world" (Revelation 12:9)? Or shall
we believe the words of Jesus, who Himself described
Satan in the Garden of Eden: " 'He was a murderer
from the beginning and does not stand in the truth,
because there is no truth in him. When he lies, he speaks
according to his own nature, for he is a liar and the
father of lies' " (John 8:44). So much for the veracity of
the ancient lie that Lucifer still spins!

But forget the lie. What is the truth Jesus declares
about death and life? " 'Our friend Lazarus has fallen
asleep, but I am going there to awaken him.' " " 'I AM
the resurrection and the life. Those who believe in me,
even though they die, will live, and everyone who lives
and believes in me will never die' " (John 11:11, 25,
26). In the face of Satan's first lie comes Jesus' last word
about death.

Which doesn't mean, of course, that if we believe in

Jesus, we will never die. After all, Lazarus did. And so will we all, if time lasts long enough. But it is very evident that the death Jesus promises we will never die is the eternal death that is the final wage of sin and rebellion (see Romans 6:23). The Bible refers to this final death as the "second death" (Revelation 20:6). Believe in Me, Jesus declares, and you will never die that forever death. For you, death will come as a quiet sleep. But I AM the Resurrection and the Life, and when I return I will awaken you one day to live with Me forever.

" 'Because I live, you also will live,' " Jesus promises (John 14:19)! The triumphant truth that shines from this radical claim is that even though death should come to you and me, it comes as a defeated foe. For through His Easter resurrection, Christ has conquered the grave. " 'Do not be afraid; I AM the first and the last, and the living one. I was dead, and see, I am alive forever and ever; and I have the keys of Death and of Hades [Greek for the grave]' " (Revelation 1:17, 18). And because He lives, we may find in Him our hope to live again too!

But a word to all those who might be thinking, *But so what? What's the big deal? What difference does it make what I believe about death?*

The answer is, It makes a very big difference! Note it carefully: If you believe, as the New Age movement teaches, that when you die, you don't really die—you go on living—then you are set up for the most destructive delusion that can come to a human being: *the appearance of spirit visitants purporting to be from the realm of the dead!*

Every month in my newspaper appears a message from Medjugorje, Yugoslavia—a message delivered by an apparition that claims to be Mary the mother of Jesus, an apparition that has been appearing daily since

June 24, 1981, to two Yugoslavian women in that village. Who is sending these messages "from within the realm of the dead"?

The truth that Jesus and the Bible teach about death means that the apparition cannot be Mary, who herself sleeps in death awaiting the return of her Son, who is the Resurrection and the Life. Then who is it that is sending these "messages," these apparitions that are now appearing with alarming frequency around the world? The biblical evidence is clear regarding the identity of the enemy of us all who would deceive the whole world! And the reason for his modus operandi is clear, for if he can deceive us into being wrong about death, in the end, we'll be wrong about life too.

And what is the truth about life? " 'I AM the resurrection and the life,' " Jesus still exclaims! Calvary's crimson stake was the site upon which the forces of life and death, light and darkness, battled for victory. But only one side triumphed in the death cry, " 'It is finished!' " (John 19:30). And by that conquest, Jesus "destroy[ed] the one who has the power of death, that is, the devil, and free[d] those who all their lives were held in slavery by the fear of death" (Hebrews 2:14, 15).

" 'I AM the resurrection and the life.' " That is not only good news about death and dying, it's wonderful news about life and living. Because the eternal life that Jesus promises *after* the resurrection actually begins *before* the resurrection!

Earlier in the Gospel of John He declared: " 'Very truly, I tell you, anyone who hears my word and believes him who sent me *has* eternal life, and does not come under judgment, but has passed from death to life' " (John 5:24, emphasis supplied). Did you notice the present tense of Jesus' promise, "*has* eternal life"?

THE CLAIM

That means that if you have accepted Jesus as your personal Saviour and invited Him to become the Lord of your life, you have the power of His resurrection life *right now*—and eternal life has already begun for you!

And did you also notice that Jesus clearly states that the one who believes in Him "does not come under judgment"? But how can that be? you may wonder. Don't the Scriptures plainly declare: "God will bring every deed into judgment, including every secret thing, whether good or evil" (Ecclesiastes 12:14)? And what about the announcement, "We will all stand before the judgment seat of God" (Romans 14:10)?

Truly, the Bible is unequivocal in its teaching about an end-time judgment. The same John who wrote the Gospel describes in Revelation a global warning to this planet just before Christ returns: "I saw another angel flying in midheaven, with an eternal gospel to proclaim to those who live on the earth—to every nation and tribe and language and people. He said in a loud voice, 'Fear God and give him glory, for the hour of his judgment has come; and worship him who made heaven and earth, the sea and the springs of water' " (Revelation 14:6, 7). The ancient prophet Daniel describes the hour of judgment with even greater detail: "The court sat in judgment, and the books were opened" (Daniel 7:10).

How, then, can Jesus promise that you will "not come under judgment" if you believe in Him (John 5:24)? The answer lies in His gift of eternal life *now!* Accept Jesus as your Saviour and trust in Him as your Lord, and your verdict in the judgment is already assured—because the Judge is on your side! " 'The Father judges no one but has given all judgment to the Son' " (John 5:22). And "there is therefore now no condemnation for those who are in Christ Jesus" (Romans 8:1)!

So let the judgment begin! For you may have the Judge on your side. And when you have Jesus, what do you have? "This is the testimony: God gave us eternal life, and this life is in his Son. Whoever has the Son has life; whoever does not have the Son of God does not have life" (1 John 5:11, 12).

Which means that even though you may die tomorrow—and you may, just as I may—death for you will come as it did for Lazarus, simply a quiet sleep. But what does it matter? Because Jesus is the Resurrection and the Life. And the New Testament rings with the blessed assurance that when He returns to this planet, He will bring with Him His resurrecting life. "For the Lord himself, with a cry of command, with the archangel's call and with the sound of God's trumpet, will descend from heaven, and the dead in Christ will rise first. Then we who are alive, who are left, will be caught up in the clouds together with them to meet the Lord in the air; and so we will be with the Lord forever. Therefore encourage one another with these words" (1 Thessalonians 4:16-18).

Wonderful and hope-filled encouragement indeed! No more fear over your "rendezvous with death"—no matter if it comes in a general hospital or by a roadside or even in your bed at home. Because when you have Jesus, you have Life . . . eternal . . . right now!

Finally, did you notice how the resurrected body of Lazarus was wrapped? "The dead man came out, his hands and feet bound with strips of cloth, and his face wrapped in a cloth. Jesus said to them, 'Unbind him, and let him go' " (John 11:44). His face was wrapped in a cloth.

Back in that time, wealthy Jews were accustomed to adorning the head of the deceased so that it could be buried exposed and appearing asleep. The poor, however, could not afford to dress the faces of their deceased, and so in order to avoid the sight of a decomposing face turning dark, the poor opted to use face cloths for their corpses.

But in a gracious act that sought to avoid shaming the poor and bring a measure of equality in the burial of the dead, the Jewish religious leaders ordered all the dead—both rich and poor—to be buried with a face cloth. And Lazarus came forth with the customary cloth bound to his face.

But notice the only other resurrection mentioned in the Gospel of John. "Simon Peter came . . . and went into the tomb [where Jesus had been buried]. He saw the linen wrappings lying there, and the cloth that had been on Jesus' head, not lying with the linen wrappings but rolled up in a place by itself" (John 20:6, 7). The contrast between the two resurrections in John is inescapable, and so is the point of their comparison! The death mask was still on Lazarus when he arose, because he would die again. But when Christ the Lord arose, the death mask was forever folded and laid aside. Lazarus's resurrection may promise hope, but Jesus' resurrection is our hope!

"I was dead, but now I am alive forevermore! For I AM the Resurrection and the Life. Those who believe in Me, even though they die, will live, and everyone who lives and believes in Me will never die" (see John 11:25, 26).

That means that in the end, there will be one goodbye that is very good news! Farewell to our general hospitals. For with Jesus, we have a rendezvous with *Life*!

CHAPTER 8

"The Bold and the Beautiful"

I AM the vine

"The bold and the beautiful" are the heroes and starlets of America's silver screen, are they not? They are the dashing men and dancing women of the Concorde jet set. And whenever Robin Leach ushers us in, ogling for a few vicarious moments the opulent lifestyles of the rich and famous, we gape at "the bold and the beautiful" sunning beside their immaculate pools or laughing amidst their gaily lighted parties. And it seems, does it not, that they are forever clutching their raised trademark wine glasses?

But are we so hungry to become as bold and as beautiful as they appear to be that we're hoodwinked and short-changed into concluding that the sparkle of the wine must be the hallmark of their affluent success? The obituaries of Hollywood and Wall Street are proof enough that the elixir of power and the secret of success do not lie in the bubbly alcohol of the aged wine. Wine never created any lasting boldness or shaped any permanent beauty.

For the fact of the matter is—the secret is in the Vine, not the wine. Discover the Vine, and the potion of power is yours for the asking.

That is precisely Jesus' radical offer in His bold declaration, " 'I AM the vine, you are the branches. Those who abide in me and I in them bear much fruit, because apart from me you can do nothing' " (John 15:5).

There it is, a tried and tested formula for sure-fire success in any life lived out in the fast track of the nineties. And it can be your secret for new power too!

A little boy was spread out on the kitchen floor, scribbling with crayons and paper. "What are you drawing?" his mother inquired as she noticed her budding artist.

"A picture of God," the boy replied.

"But, son, how can you draw a picture of God? Nobody knows what He looks like."

To which the little fellow retorted, "They will, when I get finished."

It's true, isn't it? We splash our colors and spread our crayons on the canvas of life. And almost imperceptibly, a picture of God emerges when we get finished. Our lives are not only a portrait of ourselves, but in the process of living, we have also colored a picture of God, as we perceive Him to be.

So how do you perceive Him to be? In this next to the last of the radical claims of Christ we are examining in this book, Jesus colors a new metaphor for God: "I AM the vine, you are the branches." What would happen if we sketched that portrait of Him onto the canvass of our lives? Would it become a bold portrait of new power?

Months before He spoke these words of John 15, Jesus uttered a strange and cryptic line in Luke 17.

It happened one dusty day in Palestine. The young Teacher and Healer from Galilee was crisscrossing the hillsides and villages of the land, leaving His sandal prints beside the tired, worn hearts of a people whose gloom had erased the last colors of hope from their lives. Gone were the bright greens, the flaming reds, and the royal blues. Now the national colors seemed lost in the gray and blackening shadow of failure and defeat. A foreign power held them captive. Dreams of victory were continually doused by the crush of defeat. There seemed to be no way out; they were all finished.

But not Jesus. Wherever He went, the compassionate touch of His hand and the quiet words of His heart were spreading the fresh colors of a new picture of God. To young and aged alike, He held out this new portrait with the promise that if their hearts would embrace this picture of God, it would be the beginning of a new, color-splashed way of living He called "the abundant life" (see John 10:10).

This particular day, a delegation of the religious leaders confronts the young Teacher with a burning question: When will the kingdom of God come? They are tired of waiting, tired of hoping, tired of praying, tired of losing more than winning. Their eyes are on the horizon of the future: Someday God is going to do something powerful and spectacular, and we'd like to know when.

Jesus' reply must have caught them by surprise. But when He was through, He left for us all an unforgettable portrait of God. He said, " 'The kingdom of God does not come visibly, nor will people say, "Here it is," or "There it is," because the kingdom of God is within you' " (Luke 17:20, 21, NIV).

Can you imagine that? "The kingdom of God is within *you.*" In *your* mind and *your* body, there is the kingdom of God. Oh, it's true that there is a heaven in the universe where God reigns from His eternal throne, just as the Bible teaches. As we will note in our final chapter, Jesus Himself promised to return to this planet one day to take His friends and followers to that celestial kingdom. But could it be that, like the Pharisees who came to Jesus, we have become so preoccupied with being delivered *from* this life that we have missed the divine offer for deliverance *in* this life? Could it be that in this single portrait of God that Jesus drew, we might find the golden key to unlock the door to bold divine power and bold daily victory?

Somehow, kingdom and power seem to belong together, don't they? I grew up in Japan, a land of legendary kingdoms and warlords. And I remember as a boy gazing up in awe at the rocky gray battlements and mossy stone walls that still surround the ancient pagodalike fortresses. It doesn't take much for a child's imagination to run rampant at a moment like that. Suddenly, it was as if that towering fortress of the kingdom sprang to life. I could almost see the flashing steel of samurai swords that clashed their echoes across the valley as warriors slashed with their weapons atop the castle wall. I could almost hear the curdling battle cry of the color-swathed warlords as they charged on their glistening black steeds in defense of their kingdom's citadel of power. Whether it's an aged castle in Japan or an ancient fortress in Europe, when you think of kingdom, it isn't difficult to sense the force of power.

So when Jesus describes the kingdom of God being within us, He must be offering us much more than a colorful euphemism. Talk is cheap in any language. But "the kingdom of God is not a matter of talk but of power" (1 Corinthians 4:20, NIV). And so to declare that the kingdom of God is within us is to describe a picture of incredible, infinite power! Here is a portrait of the God of all power who chooses to establish His kingdom within us. Haven't we ended the Lord's Prayer with the affirmation "For thine is the kingdom, and the power, and the glory, for ever"? And isn't power exactly what our hearts desperately need? When you think of all the shackled emotions and manacled habits that hold us captive, when you remember the vicelike grip that the win-a-few-lose-a-few "sindrome" holds on our hearts, nothing less than infinite power will do!

But the critical question our hearts desperately need to have answered is, How can I experience that kind of divine power in my life? How can I be set free from this perennial win-some-lose-some cycle that keeps falling short of victory?

Enter now Jesus' radical claim, "I AM the vine, you are the branches." Could it be we've been connected to the wrong source of power?

To find the answer, you must understand and utilize an eternal law that is operative in all human life. Solomon phrased it this way: "As he [a person] thinketh in his heart, so is he" (Proverbs 23:7, KJV). Paul expressed the same law in different words: "We all . . . beholding . . . are changed" (2 Corinthians 3:18, KJV). Both writers are describing the same law of life: *You are what you think, because what you behold you become*.

The law is true, isn't it? We have all experienced the powerful effect our thought patterns have on our behaving and our living. The simple act of watching someone else cut a fresh lemon in half and then slowly suck the sour, dripping juice into his mouth invariably produces salivation in our own mouths, doesn't it? Why? Because as our minds think *sour lemon, sour lemon, sour lemon*, the signals are strong enough to have an immediate effect on our physiological reaction to the sight of that lemon. Our tongues instantly begin to anticipate the arrival of the mouth-puckering juice of a lemon, and we start drooling!

William Parker, a Christian psychologist, powerfully illustrates this eternal law in his book *Prayer Can Change Your Life*. In it, he tells of an experiment in which a young male subject was placed under hypnosis. (While warning against the use of hypnosis, the author in this case uses it as an illustration.) The man was given a piece of chalk and was instructed to "smoke" it. Believing he was smoking a cigarette, he began to puff on that chalk. A few moments later, the researcher, feigning shock and warning, suddenly exclaimed, "Look out! It's burning your fingers." The subject immediately flung the chalk to the floor and began to complain that his fingers hurt. The researcher bandaged up the fingers, took the subject out of hypnosis, and then suggested to the man that he had burned his fingers during the experiment. He was instructed to return the next day for a physician's examination. And sure enough, when the bandages were removed, it was discovered that blisters had formed where the young man had been holding the chalk! There had been no blister before. The mind of the subject sent a signal to the body, and the body became what the mind suggested. As a person thinks, so he is; by beholding, we become changed. The law has always proven true.

In fact, research a few years ago at the National Institute of Health suggested that ailing people can get well faster by thinking positively. Candace Pert, a neuroscientist at the institute, observed, "The more I look, the more I'm convinced that emotions are running the show."

But should we be surprised? The Bible long ago declared that what we think, we are; for we become what we behold. If that is proving true for healing in the physical realm, will it not prove true for healing in the spiritual realm?

Could it be that here is a critically significant key to power-filled, successful living? As we have longed and prayed for victory over our perennial "sindrome," what, in fact, has been the focus of our thoughts? Have we been concentrating on our sins? Maybe it's an evil temper, perhaps it's sexual impurity, it might be dishonesty and unethical behavior, or maybe the problem is with jealous ego and pride. But whatever your besetting sin, have you been making it the focus of your thoughts? "O Lord, you know I have this awful sin in my life. Why, just this afternoon, I fell again. And yesterday, You remember, I had the same problem. And I know it's going to be there tomorrow when I awaken. So, Lord, take this sin away." How often have we prayed such prayers!

Certainly we can ask God to deliver us from our besetting sins. The Lord's Prayer itself petitions God, "Deliver us from evil." However, we must remember that the law we've just considered is invariable; it cannot be broken. What we think about, we are changed into; what we behold, we become. And so all these years as we've been praying for victory over that defeating sin, that sin has only entrenched itself more deeply into our subconscious as well as conscious living and thinking. Is it any wonder? We've been staring our sin squarely in the face so long that we have become what we've been beholding!

But the same law that has been our bane can become our boon! " 'I AM the vine, you are the branches. Those who abide in me and I in them bear much fruit, because apart from me you can do nothing.' " Did you catch that? "Apart from me," Jesus said, "you can do nothing."

So the secret has to be a radical shift in our daily focus, does it not? "The kingdom of God is within you." And we know "that the kingdom of God is not a matter of talk but of power." So doesn't it follow that if we will focus our thinking and our praying on the One who can install His kingdom of infinite power within us, we will experience the very power of God that we seek?

But just contemplating the words *God* and *power* or *Jesus* and *vine* can hardly be enough. It is imperative that we go to the place where that power first triumphed! Climb a rock pile called Golgotha, and gaze on that wooden cross jammed into the shaley summit of execution. That Friday two thousand years ago has much to do with this offer of freedom today. So go ahead and look long and hard at that crimson-stained Roman spike.

Stand at the cross and see the bloody, outstretched arms of God, nailed wide open in an eternal embrace, assuring us all of pardon for even our darkest sins. Let your heart become unfettered and filled with rapturous joy over the bold and beautiful gift of forgiveness that is found only at Calvary's summit.

But there is more to the death of Jesus. Not only does His cross proclaim God's *pardon*; it also promises His *power*! More than pardon for our past, God offers power for our present! More than *forgiveness* for sinning, the cross has also become a *force* for living. That's why Paul could exclaim, "The message about the cross . . . is the power of God" (1 Corinthians 1:18). That's why Peter could unequivocally declare, "He himself bore our sins in his body on the cross, so that, free from sins, we might live for righteousness; by his wounds you have been healed" (1 Peter 2:24). *The power of God is in the cross of Christ!*

How, then, can that power become yours? What did Jesus say? " 'Abide in me as I abide in you' " (John 15:4). Would you like to transform that metaphor of garden growth into living power?

Then why not try this prescription for daily power. As you awaken each morning, set aside fifteen to thirty minutes of quiet time in which you can be alone with God. Choose one of the Gospels to focus your contemplation on the life of Christ. Since each Gospel describes Jesus' pilgrimage to the cross, you will discover that wherever you turn in the Gospels you will sense the powerful shadow of Calvary. But you must not hurry through your reading. Instead, each morning select a single incident from the life of Jesus to be your focus for those contemplative moments—one story, one miracle, one parable, one teaching. Limit yourself to just one, since you want to focus clearly on the singular word of encouragement and strength the Spirit of Jesus will have for you each day.

Morning after morning as you picture the continuing scenes from the life of Jesus, you will discover the very character qualities that are the opposite of the defeating sins over which you seek victory. Focus your heart on those qualities of Jesus' life. In other words, instead of focusing on your evil temper, focus on Jesus' quiet and calm spirit, even under attack and duress at the cross. Hear Him praying under such intense and cruel provocation, " 'Father, forgive them' " (Luke 23:34). Doesn't the eternal law we've been examining state that you will become what you behold?

Or if, for example, you are seeking victory over impurity and lust, then watch Jesus carefully as you read His story and capture those moments where His character shines forth in all its transparent purity. It may be that moment we shared earlier when He stooped down beside the prostitute who had been thrown at His feet. You can tell her scarlet-stained life just by looking at her. But don't focus on your sin that you see in her. Instead, gaze into Jesus' face. See the purity that glows in His eyes. Hear again His strong words as He lifts her face to meet His: " 'Neither do I condemn you. . . . Go now and leave your life of sin' " (John 8:11, NIV). But don't hurry away. If you wish to be changed, you need time to behold. Linger in that quiet place.

Since the kingdom of God is within you, you know that at that moment He is there with you, in you. Hold that image of His purity in your mind. Thank Him for not condemning you either and for offering you His infinite power to become pure like Him. Before you leave your quiet place, picture the cross of Jesus lifted up in your mind's eye. Remember, it is not only a place of abundant pardon, but it is also a promise of abundant power! Take a moment to thank God for that power you will experience through the new day ahead, power to live Jesus' life of purity in your heart.

And then as the day wears on, bring back that picture of God revealed in Jesus. Let your mind recall what you contemplated in the early morning. Temptations will still be pounding on the lintel of your heart, but you can whisper, "The kingdom of God is within me, and it is not a matter of talk but of power. Lord, I choose to remain connected with You. Apart from You I can do nothing, for You are my Vine. Thank You for the life-giving power that is flowing into me right now." Remember, you are not to focus on your sins but rather on the infinite King within, who "is able to keep you from falling, and to make you stand without blemish in the presence of his glory with rejoicing" (Jude 24).

Once again at night, before you fall asleep, let your last prayer of the day be one of thanksgiving to God for the power He is already manifesting in your life.

" 'I AM the vine, you are the branches. Those who abide in me and I in them bear much fruit, because apart from me you can do nothing.' "

It is neither magic nor mystery. But it is a matter of power, the very power we need to live on the cutting edge of victory. The cross of Christ is eternal proof that this divine power is available to every heart that beholds Him there. "Behold the Lamb of God, which taketh away the sin of the world" (John 1:29, KJV). That's good news, isn't it? He died to take away our win-lose "sindrome." No wonder our hearts are daily summoned to behold Him there! For by beholding, we are changed. It's a matter of fact; it's a matter of power.

And isn't it a fact that your life is ready for that power now? So why not come now to the Vine and live the life of the truly bold and beautiful!

CHAPTER
9

"Days of Our Lives"

I AM the way

Cheryl Hicks's story could have come straight out of the "Days of Our Lives." For it is a story of tragedy turned to triumph turned to tragedy again. It happened in Edwardsburg, Michigan, a sleepy village a few miles down the road from mine.

Cheryl Hicks was no stranger to disaster. Just when everything was coming up roses for the young wife, her husband committed suicide. But out of her numbing grief and shock, Cheryl resolved to go on surviving. And in the process of picking up the pieces, she determined to reach out to other survivors by forming an organization of care and grief support, Michiana Survivors of Suicide, which continues to grow and flourish.

But then, that was Cheryl Hicks, always thinking of others. And the people of Edwardsburg loved her. One recalled the time Cheryl chanced upon a stranger fishing on the banks of the nearby river. When Cheryl learned that the woman was desperately fishing for her next meal, she quickly emptied her wallet on behalf of the stranger. Just because she cared. No wonder she was loved around the village.

Then came her happy marriage to Roger Hicks. And three years later their son Tyler was born. It was for little Tyler that her tragedy-turned-to-triumph story turned back into tragedy again.

It was Monday afternoon. I heard it on the news and read about it in the paper the next day. Cheryl and then three-year-old Tyler had slipped into the village post office. Inside, they bumped into neighbor Donna Proctor, and they chatted a few moments. Donna later recalled, "She was her happy and good-natured self. As she walked out she said, 'See you later.' " And then Donna heard it.

As Cheryl emerged from the post-office door with Tyler in her arms, in that freak moment, a pickup truck driven by a drunk driver careened out of control and jumped the curb onto the sidewalk. Clutching her toddler, she instantly made her decision. Her arms reflexively shot into the air, lifting little Tyler over her head. The pickup slammed into her petite body. She died instantly. Little Tyler didn't have a scratch on his body. Why? Simple. Because his mother died to save him.

And in its very simplicity, the story of Cheryl Hicks, played over and over by the local news media, became the retelling of another story long ago and faraway. The story behind Christmas and Easter and Christianity the world over. The story of Jesus of Nazareth, who gave His life to save the human race. Just like Cheryl Hicks, He . . . or should it be, just like Jesus Christ, she . . . died to save another.

Cuing in on a story like Cheryl Hicks, the Scriptures declare: "Indeed, rarely will anyone [like Cheryl] die for a righteous person—though perhaps for a good person [like Tyler] someone might actually dare to die. But God proves his love for us in that while we still were sinners Christ died for us" (Romans 5:7, 8).

And on the night before He died, Jesus turned in the flickering orange shadows of a hushed upper room to gaze into the faces of His disciples. There had been thirteen in the room moments ago. But the one who mumbled something about having a bit of business to take care of has hurried out into the night. Judas left behind twelve men—eleven disciples and one Master.

And the Master will be dead this time tomorrow evening. But nobody knows, save He. And so it is He who speaks. And when He does, He utters the second most remembered line from the Gospel of John.

The most remembered line of all Scripture is John 3:16, " 'For God so loved the world that he gave his only Son, so that everyone who believes in him may not perish but may have eternal life.' " But those other words spoken in the silence of that Jerusalem upper room—how often they, too, have been repeated!

Perhaps we ought to be grateful for the likes of Jesus' disciple Thomas. After all, he was the resident skeptic and in-house questioner of Jesus' inner circle, which would have made him a marvelous university student or professor, I am sure! But that Thursday evening, Thomas, true to form, pipes up in the middle of Jesus' great upper-room discourse, " 'Lord, we do not know where you are going. How can we know the way?' " (John 14:5).

It's evident he's still troubled by what Jesus said a moment before in answer to Peter's piqued curiosity!

> Simon Peter said to [Jesus], "Lord, where are you going?" Jesus answered, "Where I am going, you cannot follow me now; but you will follow afterward." Peter said to him, "Lord, why can I not follow you now? I will lay down my life for you." Jesus answered, "Will you lay down your life for me? Very truly, I tell you, before the cock crows, you will have denied me three times" (John 13:36-38).

And the world knows the sad story of the blustering denial that the big fisherman Peter would make later that night, just as Jesus predicted! So much for self-confident braggarts! (The good news is that if this Jesus could transform the life of Peter, then you and I can take courage with the thought of what He can do for us.)

But what under heaven can Jesus be meaning tonight, is the whispered worry that can be read on the faces of Peter and Thomas and the other nine disciples, who grapple with Jesus' cryptic words, "Where I am going, you cannot follow me now."

No doubt seeing the look of apprehension and perplexity on His disciples' lamp-lighted faces, Jesus seeks to comfort their hearts with the beloved words:

> "Do not let your hearts be troubled. Trust in God; trust also in me. In my Father's house are many rooms; if it were not so, I would have told you. I am going there to prepare a place for you. And if I go and prepare a place for you, I will come back and take you to be with me that you also may be where I am" (John 14:1-3, NIV).

Just a few weeks ago I stood on the rocky shoreline of Corregidor Island off the coast of the Philippines at the very spot where General Douglas MacArthur, under the cover of darkness, pushed away from that shell-shocked and bomb-pocked harbor fortress. Under strict orders to personally vacate the besieged island, MacArthur was secreted away through the siege lines to the safety of Australia in order to take up his command of the Pacific theater during World War II. It was from Australia that he spoke the now immortalized assurance to his beleaguered forces trapped on

Corregidor, "I shall return." And he did in triumph months later!

Two thousand years ago in that faraway upper room, Jesus made the same promise: " 'I will come again' " (verse 3). That is why, more than any other single theme, the promise of the second coming of Jesus shines with such undimmed glory throughout the Holy Scriptures. Good news for all the shell-shocked and war-weary survivors of planet Earth! No wonder it is the "blessed hope" from beginning to end (Titus 2:13)! For in the beginning, Enoch prophesied the promise of the second advent (see Jude 14), and in the end John prays the prayer of the second advent, "Even so, come, Lord Jesus" (Revelation 22:20, KJV). That is the "adventist" hope of the Bible!

But somehow Thomas misses the promise; he isn't thinking about heaven and the Father's house and Jesus returning for His followers one day. He's still trying to figure out what Jesus meant when He told Peter and the others that they couldn't follow Him to where He was going. Jesus was obviously speaking of His death, but Thomas missed the point completely. And finally, he can't stand keeping his confusion and doubt to himself, so he blurts out, " 'Lord, we do not know where you are going. [So] how can we know the way?' " (John 14:5).

"Jesus said to him, 'I AM the way, and the truth, and the life' " (verse 6). There it is, the second most well-known and repeated line from the Gospel of John and the final radical I AM claim of Jesus for our contemplation.

And no wonder it is the second most well-known of them all! For what a momentous and monumental claim Jesus makes on the eve of His crucifixion! In fact, this radical claim is the summation of all the other claims in John—I AM the Water, I AM the Bread, I AM the Light, I AM the Door, I AM the Good Shepherd, I AM the Resurrection and the Life, I AM the Vine. All of them wrapped up in—I AM the Way, the one and only Way!

Do you know what? I am absolutely convinced that Jesus is the only Way for the deepest longing in your heart and mine to ever be filled. Whatever that longing is, whatever your desire may be—emotionally, socially, physically, financially, spiritually—ultimately, Jesus is THE ONLY WAY for you, for me, and for the five billion other inhabitants of earth.

Oh, there are other ways on earth that lay claim to being *the* Way. But they are not the Way!

Hinduism is certainly not the Way. I had the privilege of spending six weeks in India last summer. This is a land with 330 million gods, which equals one god for approximately every three people. Now which one of those gods is *the* way and *the* truth and *the* life? Even an Indian will confess to you that he is not certain.

So which way is the right Way? Is it Buddhism, then—Zen or otherwise? Having been born and having grown up in Japan, I have been in hundreds of Buddhist temples and Shinto shrines. But gaze into the faces of those gods, and there is no quieting confirmation in your soul that what you have found at last is *the* Way, *the* Truth, and *the* Life.

In mentioning the great religions of the world, I do not wish to be disrespectful. But what about Islam? Is that *the* Way and *the* Truth and *the* Life the world is hungering for today? How about Judaism? While it is the cradle in which Christianity was birthed, does it offer the longing hope that will satisfy the deepest yearnings of the human race?

So where shall we turn? To the shaven-headed cult

members whom you bump into in a crowded airport concourse? Are they the ones who have found the true Way that men and women the world over are searching for?

Where is *the* Way, *the* Truth, and *the* Life today? What is it; who is it?

Is it the New Age movement? Are the great answers of life found in crystals and pyramids and tarot cards? And will all that slick and suave front for reincarnation and self-deification save a single seeking soul?

So where . . . what . . . who is the Way today?

Is materialism the answer—the incessant pursuit and possession of wealth? Haven't we seen enough of the likes of Ivan Boesky and Donald Trump to know that what Madison Avenue and Wall Street are hyping is nothing more than fool's gold? And anybody whose dominant goal in life is to make his millions will never meet his Maker at the end of that tinsel rainbow.

So where is the Way and the Truth and the Life?

It surely isn't found in the great humanistic formulas of positive and possibility thinking, is it? After all, humanism offers a rather hollow hand of help, when the guy next to you on the Long Island subway pulls out a nine-millimeter handgun and starts cutting people down. The fact is that all the positive thinking in the world isn't able to tackle the deepest moral dysfunctions of our civilization. Possibility thinking may indeed be a great way to whistle *in* the dark, but it certainly can't get you *through* the dark.

So what, then, is *the* Way, *the* Truth, and *the* Life that the world is groping for today?

Is our salvation to be found in the high-tech pantheon of science and technology? You've got to admit that the incredible feats we witness whenever our space-walking shuttle astronauts beam their images back to earth are a spectacular triumph for science and technology. But, alas, the nearly $700 million mission to save the cross-eyed and out-of-focus Hubble telescope won't help us find the focus for our own morally messed-up living back down here on terra firma! Technology will not save a single soul.

So what will? What is *the* Way and *the* Truth and *the* Life that can save this civilization?

Is it hedonism, that Budweiser philosophy of safe sex that taunts, You've got to grab all the gusto you can, because you only go through life once? So live like Hollywood . . . which thinks it lives like us! But is the pursuit of pleasure our salvation?

I was sitting in the Orlando airport enjoying a cup of hot chocolate and reading a newspaper, when a woman sat down at a table across the way. She asked for the stocks listings in the paper, so I let her borrow it. But then she wanted to talk, and I learned that she was a PA (physician's assistant) attending a convention of the American Diabetic Association.

Learning that I was a pastor, she asked if I were a Catholic priest (I thought I looked quite Protestant!). But it turned out that she wanted to confess—not for herself—but for a friend of hers she meets at these yearly conventions. A friend who is married but who lives for the hedonistic release that being away from home and husband provides her. A friend whose life mirrors the very lifestyle propagated a thousand times every day on the sets of America's soap operas, where they keep having the "days of our lives" without us! Hedonism.

But who needs an airport encounter to be reminded of the haunted, hollow hunger that ravages this nation and the nations of the world. The burned-out husks and hulls of human lives strewn along the roadside of wanton self-worship is proof enough that the pursuit of pleasure has never yet saved a single soul!

"I AM the way, and the truth, and the life," Jesus declares. And do you know what? I am convinced that He is right, that He is categorically the only Way, the only Truth, the only Life. My friends from the East suggest are many paths to the summit of the mountain. But I have found their wishful thinking to fall dangerously short of the truth. For the words of the big Fisherman still ring utterly true: " 'There is salvation in no one else, for there is no other name under heaven given among mortals by which we must be saved' " (Acts 4:12).

If you're not yet a follower of Jesus Christ, you may be saying to me, "Listen, Pastor, prove it!"

And, so, in closing, I will. I wish to prove it by describing to you the way I've seen a person die. I have had the sacred task of witnessing the death of individuals in hospital rooms, emergency rooms, bedrooms, and even along a roadside. I have seen the burning funeral pyres, and I have touched the sacred urns.

But this last spring I saw a man dying. And the reason I mention his death now is because of the profound impact his dying words had on me. I remember my friend Frank Jackson, who whispered to me before he died, "Dwight, what we need most of all is the simple message of Jesus."

A few hours later Frank died with that message of Jesus deep in his expiring heart and body. As his pastor, I know that for Frank, Jesus was truly his Way and his Truth and his Life. And in the end, that was all that mattered to him.

It has dawned on me that in the end, that is all that must matter to you and me too. "I AM the Way, the only Way," Jesus still cries out. " 'No one comes to the